I'm Worth More

I'm Worth More

Realize your value, unleash your potential

ROB MOORE

First published in Great Britain in 2019 by John Murray Learning. An Hachette
UK company.

British Library Cataloguing in Publication Data: a catalogue record for this title is available
from the British Library.
Library of Congress Catalog Card Number: on file.
ISBN: 978 1 529 35306 8
eISBN: 978 1 529 35307 5

1

The publisher has used its best endeavours to ensure that any website addresses referred to
in this book are correct and active at the time of going to press. However, the publisher and
the author have no responsibility for the websites and can make no guarantee that a site
will remain live or that the content will remain relevant, decent or appropriate.

The publisher has made every effort to mark as such all words which it believes to be
trademarks. The publisher should also like to make it clear that the presence of a word in
the book, whether marked or unmarked, in no way affects its legal status as a trademark.
Every reasonable effort has been made by the publisher to trace the copyright holders
of material in this book. Any errors or omissions should be notified in writing to the
publisher, who will endeavour to rectify the situation for any reprints and future editions.

Typeset by Cenveo® Publisher Services.

Printed and bound in Great Britain by Clays Ltd, Elcograf S.p.A.

John Murray Learning policy is to use papers that are natural, renewable and recyclable
products and made from wood grown in sustainable forests. The logging and manufacturing
processes are expected to conform to the environmental regulations of the country of origin.

Carmelite House
50 Victoria Embankment
London EC4Y 0DZ
www.hodder.co.uk

Contents

Preface

Since 2006, I've dedicated much of my life to helping aspiring entrepreneurs, freedom seekers and people who want a part- or full-time business of their own.

In the early years I thought I was helping property investors. In the middle years I thought I was helping generalist entrepreneurs. I now realize I'm helping anyone who wants to create a better life for themselves and others too.

As I reach more people, I learn more and more that we all have the same struggles and challenges. We all suffer alone despite being around so many people. We put on a brave face on social media, but things aren't always OK. We fix everyone else's problems, but struggle with our own. We are thanked for nothing yet feel responsible for everything.

I've learned that no one is immune to being crippled with the fear of failure, and never being good enough, and the seemingly constant judgement and criticism and ridicule, and the crises of confidence, and the battling with your own demons.

There is nothing wrong with you. This is part of being human. There are reasons and seasons. This is part of being an entrepreneur, a risk taker, a creative, an artist and someone who cares for others.

I believe the world needs to know and understand the balanced view of success, fulfilment and self-worth. The paradox of always striving for more; to grow, to be better, yet to be content and happy with who and where you are now. To drive, strive, but also feel alive.

My work has taken on higher levels of abstraction and reach, from property to business to time management to self-worth, but there is one consistent, constant theme throughout, and that is how we all value ourselves. Our self-perception, self-worth and dare I say it, self-love.

You can't charge fair and meaty fees for your products and services if you don't believe in yourself. You can't sell if there's a hole in your soul. You can't put yourself out there if there's something wrong in there. Underlying every business, every pitch, every sale, every start-up, every side hustle, every invest-ment, every partnership, every job role, and every relationship is how you feel about yourself. If you realize your value you can unleash your potential.

My job is not just to write from my own experience, though this is what I've always done. I've never written a 'research pro-ject', I've always written about what I've learned and earned and struggled with and succeeded in myself. Because my experiences as an entrepreneur, freedom seeker, go-getter, big believer, naive unrealistic thinker are the same as everybody else's, I am able to write a book from true and deep experience, that is also needed by many. I don't write for myself, I write for my communities, followers and fans. And "how do I realize my value and unleash my potential" is the common recurring question I get asked over and over again.

Could this be the book of all my books that does the most good? Could this be the book that takes my own struggles and challenges and occasional victories, and helps you solve and create your own? Could this be the book that helps you feel not so alone, not so lacking in skills and experience and confidence, not so lost?

I hope so. I thank you deeply for following me on your journey; for allowing me to come with you on this epic ride. Because you are worth so much more. You know it, maybe you just need my help to show it.

PART I
Introduction

I

(False) idols

One of my all-time idols is Arnold Schwarzenegger.

Pretty much from birth I was raised living in pubs. My parents worked very long, late hours. To keep me entertained (quiet), Mum used to take me to Blockbuster and rent me a film. I always wanted the 18s (because I was about 11) and occasionally talked Mum into getting me an Arnie film.

Other than the fact that I was too young to be watching them, I loved all the Arnie films. Even the dodgy ones. I looked up to him. He made me want to be a superhero. I had no idea he'd also won Mr Olympia so many times. I had no idea he would make millions in real estate, or that he'd sell millions of books, or become the Governor of California. I just wanted to be more like him. I even started to lift weights, which, if you've seen me now, you'd know didn't quite work out.

For nearly 25 years I put Arnie on a pedestal. He could walk on water; he was an alchemist who turns everything he touches into gold. My guru, above me, up there – a place I'd surely never reach.

The older I became, the less empowered I felt about it. For a decade, the admiration was motivating. It inspired me to want to be greater myself. It lifted me up. But over the years I started to feel unworthy. How would I ever reach those heights? He was born that way, I wasn't. I'm never going to be that great. It started to have the opposite effect. It was like it picked and pecked and nagged away me; a constant reminder of all the things I had not achieved. The person I wanted to be, but never could reach.

And then I met the man himself.

I was very nervous. I felt like a silly fan boy. I felt unworthy and small. I rehearsed over and over what I was going to say, analysing every word. I imagined his response to everything I said, and came up with the perfect script that would make me look the least goofy. I repeated it a couple of times in my head just before we were in the same room, alone, held my breath, and then … in he walked.

Wow. He's way shorter in real life (was my immediate thought). That's because I'd imagined he was 7 foot 10, like André the Giant.

As we shook hands, I could see the top of his head. *Wow. He dyes his hair, too.*

This completely threw me. Had it shattered my dreams of the perfect superhero? Or did I all of a sudden feel better about myself? After all, the great Arnie isn't 'perfect' either.

We spent the next 30 minutes together. Unsurprisingly, he was lovely. He even seemed a bit nervous around someone he didn't already know. Or maybe my nervousness made him nervous? I don't know, but most strikingly, he was totally, utterly and completely normal.

Arnie was the height that Arnie always was, and is. OK, perhaps he's shrunk an inch or two. Even the great Arnie shrinks with age. And of course he dyes his hair; he's nearly 70. I'd dye my hair at 70.*

Just like I'd made him a foot taller *in my head*, I'd set him on a pedestal way up high above me, as if everything about him was out of reach. He was consummate and impeccable. But just

---

* I have no proof he dyes his hair; it just looked that way. Or maybe I expected it to be perfectly black.

as your entire life can flash by you in near-death moments, it hit me all at once: I made *everything* about a man I'd never even met a (false) vision of perfection.

Not only was that unhealthy for my own self-worth, as I unconsciously compared and (de)positioned myself against him, it was also factually incorrect. The entire time I spent with Arnie played out absolutely nothing like the script I'd practised in my head. And years on, do you think Arnie thinks day and sleepless night how much of a goofball I was? OK, don't answer that.

Can you see what I did there? If you've ever done anything like this anywhere in your life, in your own way, then this book will help get it, and you, out of the way, so you can get on your way. This book is here for you if you've ever:

- compared yourself to anyone, only to feel empty and unworthy
- worried about things, your abilities, and made them bigger or worse than the reality
- felt that you don't have the 'born talents' of the people you admire or idolize
- felt that you could or should be much more, but aren't where you want to be
- felt lost, had low self-worth and talked yourself down and out of things
- undercharged, or feel that your fees, income or salary should be (much) higher
- beat yourself up about mistakes, failings and things in the past
- felt that you are not living up to others' expectations of you
- felt that you are not living up to *your own* expectations of you

- felt that you don't deserve success, happiness or wealth
- felt weak, useless or alone.

Is Arnie flawless, faultless and beyond compare?

No. He is simply great at being Arnie. And you are great at being you. Arnie has mastered and now *owns* his *own* talents and uniqueness.★★ This book, *I'm Worth More*, will guide you to discover, honour and then unleash your own skills, talents and gifts *unique* to you – not compared to or modelled on anyone else, but the version of you that you know you can be. The version of you that you already are, but aren't valuing (enough, yet). The version of you that you aren't showing the world (enough, yet).

The world needs to see it, but first you have to be it. And to be it, you have to believe it. I would like to help you see what's already there, in you, and to help you see in yourself what you see in your idols.

★★ I bet if you asked Arnie whether he thought he was perfect, you'd find he has insecurities and fears too, like you.

2

What is real?

I used to think that Radiohead was the best band in the world, and that everything else was inferior. You can see why I didn't have many friends. I used to think that, if you didn't find *South Park* funny, there was something wrong with you. I used to think it should be made illegal to support Manchester United. OK, I am right some of the time.

When I was young I wanted to be a professional golfer. I'd long before convinced myself I was the unluckiest golfer who'd ever lived. Every time there was a competition I was playing, there would be a strong headwind when it was my turn to stand on the first tee. That headwind would only blow when I was playing, and on the back nine the wind would change 180 degrees and blow back in my face like the front nine.

Just telling you this makes me feel so ignorant and naive. But for 26 years of my life I was convinced that how *I saw things* were how they were. That my perception was *the* reality. That there was only *one* reality. That everyone else was wrong, not me. People would only 'understand' when they saw the world *my* way; the only way, the *right* way.

Well I was right, and I was wrong. So *very* wrong. This next part, only shown to me 26 years into my life, is one of the most simple, yet profoundly life-changing concepts I've learned in my life:

- There is no one, single reality.
- There is only an individual perception.

- An individual's perception forms the individual's reality.
- Reality is only perception turned into individual reality.
- Reality is projection of an individual's perception.

You can summarize this all in this one short sentence:

Reality is malleable, not fixed. You can create your reality.

In 2006, my breakthrough year of self-education, I attended a lot of personal-development seminars. Many of them made this claim about malleable, infinite realities; perceptions projected out to become individual realities. It was a mind-bender to me. How can there not be a single, fixed reality?

I held on to my single reality (that only my reality was *the* reality) tightly at first. It makes sense that I would; it's my reality being questioned and shattered. I wasn't the only one who wrestled with this concept. My business partner, Mark Homer, and I debated passionately (argued) about this:

Me: Reality is only an individual's perception and therefore malleable.

Mark: There has to be one, single, fixed reality.

Me: But individual perception changes it.

Mark: No, the individual might see it differently, but it is single and fixed.

Me: No, because the individual seeing it changes it.

Mark: No, there *has* to be one, single, fixed reality.

Me: But, Mark, individual perception changes it.

Mark: NO! The individual might see it differently, but it is single and fixed.

Me: NO, because the individual seeing it changes it.

Twelve years later we are still having the same debate. Twelve years later and Mark is still wrong.

Now you may accept that reality is perception, or you may believe that there is a single, fixed reality that we all perceive differently. To me, it doesn't matter. As long as you believe that your reality is as you see it, not as it is. And, even more importantly, that your reality is malleable, and can be changed by *you*. You have the power to change your own reality by changing your perception. Instantly, as you change your perception, you change your entire reality. You can literally become an alchemist of a new, desired reality through open-minded vision and decision.

And you can do the same with your self-worth. Your self-worth is not fixed. It doesn't matter what your parents told you, how you were raised, where you failed or what scars and baggage you carry with you. It doesn't matter how long ago these events that shaped you took place. It doesn't matter how painful they were or how deeply rooted they are. Your self-worth is malleable because it is only *your* perception of you. Even if people around you have been telling you that you're not good enough your entire life, it is your choice what you believe about yourself.

Even your self-worth isn't real. It is your own illusion of who you are, as perceived by you. Others may see you differently, either as a greater version of you – those supportive people who see more in you than you see in yourself – or as a lesser version – those who look down on you or don't believe in you.

These outer perceptions aren't real either. They are simply an individual's perception, projected out and on to you. Be very careful and selective of the reality you create, from the reality others have created then projected on to you.

Once we create the illusion of perception, we create our inner and outer reality. We then make it mean something. Human beings seem to have the desire, even need, to make everything *mean* something. To figure out the meaning of life. To figure out the meaning of our own life. Our purpose. Why we do things. Why others do things.

This critical thinking is a vital life survival aid. If you are a parent, you will know that one of the most annoying words your kids repeat over and over and over, is 'Why?'. Mummy, why? Mummy, why? Mummy, why? Mummy, why why why?

As a human being, your survival is not guaranteed. The taking for granted of your safety would likely end in death. On a primal level, some things help ensure your survival and some things threaten it. You need to be able to work out which one it is, very quickly and clearly.

Early in life, having loving, caring parents makes us feel our survival is secure. Having parents who do not love or care about us (or if we perceive that to be the case) makes us feel our survival is threatened. As an adult, external events either better ensure or threaten our survival (either in reality or in our perception).

This 'meaning-making' faculty hardwired into our brains drives a default view of everything that happens around us, and as we perceive it. That might manifest itself in a recognition of a real, clear and present danger, fear of public speaking, how others will judge us, or our general self-worth. The need to discover and judge an event's likely impact on us influences us to look for meaning in everything; even events that have no inherent or singular meaning at all. Which is *all* events, because reality is only perception. Reality exists in the mind, not in the world.

Because events have no meaning, events that you perceive damage your self-worth are not real either. You put a meaning on external events and people, because you are looking to ensure your survival. Then you make these events mean something they don't actually mean. As humans, we tend to be negatively biased, as this better ensures our survival than being relaxed or complacent, attitudes which can arise from more positive bias.

This all carries over into your self-perception and self-worth. You make these non-events far more critical and damaging than they actually are, which serves your survival but not your happiness, fulfilment and inner feeling of being good enough. This can also happen in reverse, where your self-worth is aggrandized. This book, though, is called *I'm Worth More*, not *I'm Worth Less*, so we won't be looking at this, more unusual, case here. Cocky bastards needn't read this book.

What this book will address is how to see the *real impact* of events and people on your self-worth, the meaning you're giving them that's then driving how you feel about yourself, and how to change the meaning. The change of meaning then changes the reality instantaneously, and you become an alchemist of higher self-worth and value. You literally create your higher self-worth reality by understanding how you are creating meaning, and how to create new, more realistic, balanced or empowered meanings from the same events that previously damaged you.

We all have this innate ability; I would like to help you bring it out. You are not broken or damaged; you just need to change your perception which instantly changes your reality. You just need to see what's already there but you are filtering out, like people giving you compliments that you never hear or believe, or when you never noticed a car on the road until you bought one, when it suddenly seemed that everyone had one.

3
My hippiest book yet?

Sit somewhere comfortable. Familiar. Alone. Close your eyes. Relax. Breathe in through your nose, and out through your mouth. In for four seconds. Out for five. That's right. Just like that. Focus just on your breathing. If thoughts come into your head, simply notice them, then let them go, like waves washing against the shore.

No!

STOP!

Really?

Did you *really* think this was where this book was going to go? Puh-leaze. *But,* a book about self-worth might not be what you'd expect from an entrepreneur. We tend to prefer different methods. It's less about meditating away your problems and manifesting your millions than hustling, right?

Taking massive action. Isn't success all about the grind? Aren't lunch and sleep for wimps? Don't you just have to work hard AF and hashtag it 10×?

Hell, yeah.

Well, no, actually.

You wouldn't waste time trying to fill a bucket with a hole in it. You wouldn't turn the water on faster. You wouldn't shout at the water for running through the hole. Water, will you STOP escaping FFS.

No.

You'd plug the hole.

Since 2006 I've been building property portfolios and businesses for myself, with my business partners, and helping my communities do the same. Back then, I naively thought that giving people good information would be enough to help them succeed. After all, knowledge is power, right? Again, no.

I soon learned that if that were the case, if it were that easy, then everyone would learn–do–succeed. I learned that motivation to act was also required. But the problem with motivation is that it's like plugging the hole in the bucket with straw. It might work for a fill or two, but then it will leak, and soon it will break.

I then learned that inspiration – a deeper alignment of the strategy to one's own values – was more lasting. But even with a deep desire and passion, without a foundation of empowered identity, beliefs and self-worth, any strategy would be built on sand, and in the end the waters would wash away the castle.

I never intended to write books on 'starting now and getting perfect later' or 'self-worth'. I intended to write strategy 'how to' books, like my property, leverage and money books. But having taught and guided hundreds of thousands of people for more than a decade, I'd have to be an idiot not to spot the common resistance points along the journey for investors, entrepreneurs, career hunters, parents, side-hustlers and self-improvers. And those resistance points were not what I expected, and perhaps not what I wanted to admit (to myself).

Think about the logic of getting any kind of discount on anything. It's not that hard to get 20 or 25 per cent off the asking price or value of a property, for example. Simply get on Rightmove, check every relevant property listed, call up the estate agents, book the viewings, then offer 30 per cent below market value on every deal that you see. Offer enough and BANG!, you'll get your deal. Then track the numbers, and scale up.

If you get one deal every 25 offers, then you'd get four deals every 100 offers. If you do 100 offers every year, you'd get four 20–25 per cent below-market-value deals every year. That's 40 in a decade. There you go – financially free. Easy AF. Bosh.

You could do the same for watches, cars, shoes, travel, groceries, stationery … pretty much everything you buy. So, why don't you? Might I suggest:

- fear of rejection
- fear of looking stupid in front of others
- a lack of belief that the seller would sell at a discount (even though you know the 'numbers game')
- a fear of the negotiation process and/or upsetting someone
- the feeling that you don't deserve the extra money/ discount
- the feeling that you're taking money from someone else.

These are the holes in the bucket. No matter how much sales or marketing or negotiation or strategy training one does, it won't fill the hole. It will simply pour more water into the bucket. That's a very expensive bucket. In fact, it's often a convenient way to convince yourself you're making progress – by busily procrastinating and avoiding the real issues. I'll just keep filling the bucket with water and hope that it will fill itself.

The cosmetics industry thrives off this. People pay vast amounts of money to hide or augment areas of their body they don't like (or haven't learned to value). Rarely do bigger lips, hips or breasts give lasting happiness and self-love. They merely feed an addiction to buy more and bigger, which creates a vicious cycle of temporary pleasure over more lasting acceptance, contentment … even happiness. Women are putting implants in their asses and men in their biceps. Otherwise smart people are putting their health at risk to look good to others (when often they don't look good; they have an addictive delusion). Instead, learning how to value who they are and what they have already is where they really need to put the effort in.

People get addicted to 'likes' on social media. They crave the thumbs-up to fill their inner voids. God forbid if no one comments, or, worse, gives them a thumbs-down; the world as we know it is doomed. If anyone dares to critique a post, then a full-scale Jerry Maguire-style flip-out follows.

To gain approval or love, or the self-worth they can't achieve within themselves, people will:

- buy things they can't afford for (and to impress) people they don't really like
- make people laugh to hide their own insecurities, as is often the case with comedians
- talk badly of, criticize and talk down others to elevate themselves
- take on other people's problems and become a martyr
- avoid saying no, and get themselves into situations that make them unhappy
- constantly seek the approval, agreement or permission of others
- take any kind of criticism badly and personally
- over-apologize and take the blame for things they don't need to
- judge, blame, complain, self-justify or play the victim
- hide away, play small and stand back for fear of ridicule
- go with the consensus and change their mind on a whim to 'fit in'.

If you have low self-worth, specifically related to any of the behaviours or fears in this chapter so far, then no matter how much you try to make money, or how much money you make, you won't hold on to it. No matter ...

- how much you make others laugh, you will never feel enough inside
- how much you talk badly of others, you will never feel good about yourself
- how many times you play the martyr, you will never become your own hero
- how many times you avoid saying no, you will never be able to say yes to yourself
- how much approval or permission you get from others, you will never please yourself
- how many times you apologize, you will never forgive yourself
- how much you blame and complain, you will never take responsibility
- how much you stand back, you will never step up.

No matter how many courses you go on, or business models you research or juggle, or how late you work in the office or the diets you try, unless you fill your self-worth void, you will never feel whole.

No matter how much water you pour into the bucket, it will never fill up unless you plug, then fix the hole.

I wrote this book because it transcends all other books I have written. Because property investing, entrepreneurship, raising cash, building teams, partnerships, parenting, careers, general success and happiness all start from within.

This is still an action-oriented book, so don't worry, I haven't completely lost the plot. The main themes in this book are more common and experienced by more people than my other books combined to date. Not everyone wants to buy a property, or make money (I know, weirdos), but everyone wants to feel better about themselves and that they are worthy of all the things they desire.

All the battles I've had with myself, and the experience I've gained from thousands of hours of coaching and mentoring others, are written into *I'm Worth More*. This book (and your self-worth) can be the cornerstone and bedrock of everything you want to do, be and have in your life.

Now uncross your legs, open your eyes, roll up your mat and let's do this!

4

Value vs. worth

Value and worth are not the same. In the interests of your self-worth, the semantics *do* matter. In society generally, 'value' is defined as, and used in the sense of, 'personal importance at a specific time'. 'Worth' is defined as, and used in the sense of, 'cost' of a particular thing, or the 'greatness' or financial status of a particular person.

On a personal, internal level, value is the external manifestation of your inner worth. After all, self-worth isn't called 'self-value'; it's called self-worth. Things that you value, such as material items, your home or career, are all outside of yourself. Even family and experiences are all external to your inner being.

- Value is an external projection; worth is an inner perception.
- Value is market forces; worth is what your self reinforces.
- Value is reflexive; worth is introspective.
- The difference matters.
- Do not let the outer doubter define the inner winner.

Value is the external position and price you attach to something – a product, service or pitch – based in your inner self-worth. Value is malleable, but inner worth must be fixed (or increased). If inner worth is low, or variable, outer value will follow suit. You can't price something competitively, or even expensively, if your inner worth is paltry.

If you 'value' yourself, your 'worth' will increase. If you don't, or you de-value yourself, your worth will decrease, or not exist in the first place. I've written this book to help you:

- increase your inner self-worth, and so …
- … dictate and drive up the manifested value in your life
- value who and what you already have
- go *more* for what you desire to have
- become who you'd like to be – someone you'd admire
- increase your prices, salary, earnings and business (see Part 6)
- revalue yourself when your self-worth has been damaged
- know the important difference between a mistake and a deeper issue
- attract and retain the right people into your life
- have the courage to reject and remove the wrong people
- have better information and meaning to measure your true self-worth
- get worth from who you are, not from what others think of you
- stop doubting, worrying, comparing or, worse, beating yourself up
- stop the loop of low self-worth pushing people and success away from you.

When you don't value yourself, it's hard to value, or see value, in anything else. Therefore, inner self-worth and outer perceived value, while fundamentally different, are inextricably linked and reflexive. One directly affects the other, and vice versa.

It is relatively easy to attach outer value, or even worth, to something material. The market forces, competition and comparison all give frames of reference to attribute a concrete (perceived) value to something. However, the worth *you* attach to it could vary. You might want to pay less because you deem it is worth less *to you*. Or you could pay an over-the-market-price because it has a higher worth to *you*.

But to do the same for your inner self-worth, that's altogether different. There are no other *you*s that exist. There are no other frames of reference. There are no market forces governing your inner self-worth. There is only your self-image; how you see and speak to yourself. Self-worth is entirely subjective. It is a perception that isn't a reality, but becomes *your* reality. Some self-worth resistance may not be your fault, but if you want to improve it, it is your responsibility to manage and change it. And you can.

People will spend much time, money and effort avoiding the deeper causes, in the hope that something external will save them. A new course. A new dog. A new partner. A new outfit. Another holiday. A new area to live. Not only do these not change anything meaningful, at least not for any enduring amount of time, they can create cyclical addictions to the temporary relief they provide. Each time the temporary pleasure subsides, it exposes ever deeper compounding issues.

I'm Worth More not only calls out all those peripheral distractions and deceptions, but it will help you get to the root cause of the area(s) of your life in which you'd like to feel more worth(y). Contrary to generic popular opinion – that people either have high self-worth or low self-worth – *everyone* has high self-worth in the specific areas of their life they have focused, honoured, mastered or been raised well in. Yes, everyone. But, *everyone* also has low self-worth in the areas they have disowned, failed, not focused on, or been subjected to poor parental or societal influence in.

Even Arnie, my perfect hero.

I also don't want to scare off anyone who doesn't feel like their overall self-worth is at an all-time low. While this book will help people who have generally low confidence and self-worth, it will help anyone who wants to increase it overall, like a millionaire who wants to become a deca-millionaire or billionaire. Or someone who once had charisma and confidence, but something has happened to make them feel like they've lost it. Or someone who has it in many areas, but can't quite work out why they don't have it in one particular desired or new area.

Just because no one made you feel valuable doesn't mean you are worthless.

Just because you made one mistake, or many, doesn't mean you are a failure.

Just because you have low worth in one area of your life doesn't mean you have it in all areas of your life. You may not value yourself as much as you could, but you are worth significantly more.

5

How we value anything and everything

There is only one way to value something, or anything. That is by comparing it to something else. The perception of value cannot exist in a vacuum, as if it has no frame of reference or relevance.

How would you know that white was white unless you could compare it to black? How would you know pleasure unless you could compare it to pain? How would you know poverty unless you knew, or understood, the concept of wealth?

This frame of comparison is very beneficial for external value. It makes it easier and quicker to compare value, price and relative utility. You can ascertain the market value.

You perceive something to be a bargain if you feel you've paid less than it is worth. You feel stitched up or ripped off if you feel you've paid more than it is worth. You only feel (know) this because you have a perception of relative worth. That worth is also subjective. You could pay less than something is valued at, because it is worth less to you than it is to the market. You could also pay more than something is valued at, but to you it seems worth paying more for.

I was born in 1979. I love watches. So, one of the most valuable watches to me is the '79 Rolex Daytona. I'm almost as vintage as these watches now. In addition to the Daytona's market value, it has my birth year and life-worth-value added in. I will be passing these to my children too, which adds even more value to me. I had better not make this information too public otherwise sellers will catch on to this increased worth (to me), and price it in (up).

This is the reflexive, subjective nature of external perceived value. The same goes for your inner self-worth. You can value yourself higher or lower than anything, relatively. This relativity could be you comparing yourself to someone else, or where you were in the past, or where you'd like to be in the future. You could compare yourself to an ideal defined by society or the media, or through the lens of a perfectionist complex or impostor syndrome.

The market has no emotion. It simply has its forces of demand and supply, competition, regulation and so on. All these are quite measurable. You, on the other hand, have far more complexities and influences. It is my aim to give you tools, either new, or already within you, to help you measure and master your self-worth more quantifiably. More like a market than a mystery. More against yourself than comparing to others. More intrinsically driven than externally influenced.

Would you feel better about yourself, more valuable and worthy, if you stopped:

- the comparison curse: comparing yourself to others (unfavourably)
- comparing where you are to where you perceive you *should* be
- letting the mainstream and social media image impact your self-worth
- blaming someone or something for what happened to you in the past
- being influenced by the wrong people who don't lift you up
- trying to be someone you are not so as to please people you don't like

- being scared that you don't deserve it, or that it might all be taken away, or that you'll get 'found out'
- letting things people say affect how you feel about who you are.

To stop yourself doing one, any or all of these, you need to follow the 'triple A' process:

1 **(Be) aware:** Gain awareness, and then mastery, of your emotions.
2 **Accept:** It is how it is meant to be. You can't change it. Discover new facts about yourself that you're not yet seeing that help you accept this.
3 **Act:** See balance in any situation (the upside to the downside, or vice versa). Then do something positive and proactive about it.

This will be the foundational process for you to stress-test any situation that challenges your self-worth. There's more on this later, but first here's a more important question than 'What is the value of anything?' – 'What is the value of something, to *you?*'

6

How *you* value something

Just like external value is subjective, so is your inner value, and what you value, and your values. What you value is determined by your *values*. Your values are the things personal and unique to you, that you believe and hold to be most important in your life. They are principles you live by and act upon, which drive your beliefs and behaviours.

Your values are completely unique to you, because you are unique too. No two human beings are the same, not even identical twins, according to many scientific studies of DNA, genomes, neurology and axiology.

Before I dive into this, I feel it's both important to attempt to prove and back up the individual uniqueness of you as an individual, but also not to unnecessarily drown you in science. The purpose of my desire to prove your uniqueness is to show you the following:

- We are all unique, and therefore the very best in the world at being ourselves.
- We are all necessary and useful to society, and have a unique place of value.
- If a genius is defined as someone who is the very best, then you are a genius too.
- We therefore all have equal worth, and our self-worth should/can back that up.
- We have every reason to have high self-worth and have no one to compare ourselves to.

Let's start with some quick research, then move quickly into the relevance to you. It is widely accepted that no two human beings have the same DNA or genetic make-up. There are more than 3 million differences in your genomes to other people's, despite 99.9 per cent of it being the same, according to Genome News Network. It used to be thought that identical twins had exactly the same genetic make-up, until recent research suggested that even identical twins do not have the exact same genetic make-up.*

According to research by scientists at the Stanford University School of Medicine and Yale University, the key to human individuality and uniqueness lies in the sequences that surround and control our genes. The interaction of those sequences with a class of key proteins, called transcription factors, can vary significantly between two people and are likely to affect our appearance, our development and even our predisposition to certain diseases.

So, genetically, it appears that we are all different. Bear with me for the importance and relevance of this to your self-worth.

Axiology is the study of values and value. The origin of axiology is *axios*, Greek for 'worth'. It seeks to understand the nature of values and value judgements. It seeks to answer the questions of 'why?' and 'how come?'. It seeks to understand what motivates us to take or hold off from actions. The difference between humans and other living things is that humans seek value beyond self-preservation. They seek to value and understand the meaning of beauty, truth, love. You could call these spiritual values. Just as no two people have the same exact genetics, no two people value exactly the same things equally or to the same extent.

---

* The 1000 Genomes Project Consortium, 2008–2015 and Identification of individual subjects on the basis of their brain anatomical features. Scientific Reports, 4 April 2018.

Neurology and studies of the brain have shown that our brains react very differently from others in exactly the same situations. Studies on how music affects the brain, by scientists at the University of Southern California, examined the brain scans of students. Half of the students had intense reactions to music, and half didn't. One respondent believed her body completely changed when she listened to the song 'Nude' by Radiohead. The studies showed that each individual reacted to the music differently, and that everyone has a totally different set of molecules in the brain that makes us all unique.

If we add to genetics, neurology and axiology, parenting, environment, culture, media, friends and social influences, it's easy to see just how hard it would be to be the same as someone else. We have a completely unique make-up, life and individual experiences that shape each and every one of us as a totally unique, one-off, one-of-a-kind individual.

That is pretty special if you ask me. That is a miracle. What are the odds?

Well, 400 trillion to one, according to Mel Robbins, author of *The 5 Second Rule*.

When our self-worth is low it is very easy to forget this. Instead of feeling as special as we really are, and grateful for the statistical miracle just to be alive, day by day little (and big) events and the things people say chip away at the special, unique human being that we are and grind us down. We feel at best normal, or like a rat in a race or a hamster in a wheel. Our thinking closes and our perception narrows. We start to believe what people say about us, things that don't serve us or aren't about who we really are. We allow perceived mistakes to begin to gnaw away at our inner self-worth until we are so far removed from the unique and special human we all started out being. Instead of flourishing and self-actualizing, we stymie ourselves. We rarely do this consciously, it just sneaks up on us as we deal with all the threats to our being.

Feeling special and unique, both factually as presented in this chapter, and emotionally about ourselves, are vital ingredients of self-worth. You don't have to become special to increase yourself worth; you just have to remember that you *are* special.

I believe there is a purpose for us all being unique. The main reason links to the interdependent nature of our species. We require one other for survival. We need love, but we also need utility and amenity. All the things that you need day to day are created by someone else. All the things you consume are produced by someone else. The things you create or produce are consumed by someone else. You give value and receive value. Everyone gives value and receives value. It's a fine, delicate, elegant balance. If we all valued the same things in the same manner, we would not serve and be served in all the areas essential for our survival.

Without uniqueness, we would all do the same things, and no one would do all of the other things. Too many cooks wouldn't just spoil the broth, but they would create an abundance of soup and a lack and scarcity of everything else. Our species would not be able to survive with lots of soup and nothing else.

I am less concerned about the science and evolution, and more concerned about the relevance to you. But first, you need to believe me that you are unique. That you are just as special as anyone else, even Arnie. That you are *supposed* to be you. Your strengths and your flaws. Your gifts and your struggles. Your mistakes and your imperfections. Once you believe that – and forgive me if I have banged on too long about it – then you can start to see how it is of great benefit, value and worth to be you. How people actually need you, like you need them. How people look up to you, like you look up to them.

Then your first challenge becomes how to discover that uniqueness in you. Many people think that it isn't in them. That it is a mystery that someone else holds or is born with. But this isn't the case. It is already in you.

Your next challenge is to own it. Then work it, baby. Show it to the world. Parade it. Then monetize it, if that's the outcome you want. Welcome to *I'm Worth More.*

In Part 6 we will look at converting your own uniqueness into monetary form. The reality is that you are already a millionaire, deca-millionaire or billionaire, but in another form. In a latent, non-monetary form. You might be a millionaire parent, deca-millionaire yoga instructor or a billionaire cook. The billionaire has converted their own values and uniqueness into monetary form, and you can, too.

I sometimes lose people at this stage, because they think that it is easier for some to convert their values based skills into money. *It's OK for the real estate or tech guys and girls, but what about me and my little niche? I can't convert knitting or hot dog selling into millions, can I?* Well, let's see about that.

Frank Warren started a business called Post Secret, where he would ask people to send him postcards with their secrets written on the back. After gathering up other people's secrets, he turned them into books and has been at the top of the best-seller list five times and made millions.

There was a very popular website called MyExcusedAbsence.com that offered a number of excuse letters like doctor's notes and jury summons. It didn't take much for the owner of the website to get started, just a laptop and $300, but he made a hell of a fortune selling these excuses for $25 a pop.

In 2005 student Alex Tew needed a way to pay for college. He created a website called the 'million-dollar homepage'. A one-page website, with exactly 1 million pixels. He (quickly) sold the pixels for a dollar each. Within a matter of months, he made a cool $1 million.

Kim Lavine designed a microwaveable pillow called the Wuvit, which completely changed the financial situation of her family. Before she decided to give her idea a go, her husband had just lost his job and there was absolutely no income in their household. But that changed pretty fast, as she managed to earn nearly a quarter million dollars in the first eight weeks of starting her business. Yes, a microwaveable pillow.

I could share many more stories like this. In fact, I shared some in my book *Money* to prove that you can make money out of virtually anything, and big money, too. There will be more of these stories later in the book to both prove and inspire you that you can monetize your passion, profession and areas of highest value.

These stories are not as rare as you might think. They are simply an example of what we all do: focus on what we value the most. Find our own uniqueness in the practice and pursuit of our specialism. Express our individuality though our passions and professions in a unique way that we personally value. These people have just monetized their uniqueness by converting what they value into something someone else will value. And you can, too.

The value of anything, material or immaterial, to you is determined through its ability to provide you with positive emotions, which are the feedback to the value you perceive. These emotions could be happiness, the feeling of progress and completion, importance, or fulfilment. You will get more of these emotions, and thus your self-worth will increase, when you pursue things of value to you, that have value to others, and so act as a virtuous feedback loop.

How you value something, anything, is unique to you because you are unique. Value is subjective to you because it is subjective to all. We all project our values, and what is most important to us, on to others, in an attempt to make them more like us or agree with us. People measure us by their own standards, not our own. Our self-worth can rise and fall based on how we perceive others perceive and value us. Strong self-worth comes from knowing what you value, and that you have value, and owning the unique value that you bring to the world.

7
Where self-worth comes from

If you can find the specific source from where your self-worth originates, then this can give you valuable information to start building it (back) up. This subject is a bit of a minefield, because you can pick up things that form your beliefs in so many different areas of your life that you attach to your inner feeling of worth. Many stem from your childhood where much of your personality and beliefs are formed, but many also arise through significant (emotional) events along your life's journey.

It is important to be able to recognize where much of your self-worth originated. Not just areas of low self-worth you'd like to improve, but areas of strong self-worth you'd like to model. I see self-worth like a battery gauge that can go from fully charged to one bar left, to about to die on you, to fully charged again. It tends to be dynamic, not static, based on your perception of events.

Here are some areas from where your self-worth has originated. These are influences that shape what you believe to be true, about the world and yourself relative to your environment. It could be one main driving factor or a combination of many. As you read through these, note the ones that you perceive have affected you:

- childhood and parenting (parents or single parent, guardian, divorce)
- society (culture, geographic location; permanent or variable)

- schooling (teachers, results, status and peers)
- love (received or not received from parents, family and friends, especially as a child)
- peers and social groups (authority figures, comparing yourself to them)
- media influences
- your body image (appearance, eating, peers and social/media influences)
- your personal achievements (or perceived failures)
- finances (upbringing, money beliefs, status)
- sexual and romantic experiences and relationships
- trauma, abuse, bullying, addictions and disorders
- strong emotional experiences and events (positive and negative)
- rejection and criticism
- guilt and shame of perceived mistakes and bad decisions
- expectations and comparisons
- self-talk (how you talk to yourself about all of the above)
- what other people say about you.

The meaning that you have placed on these above influences, whether they better secure or threaten your being, have formed your self-worth and how you feel about yourself. Later in *I'm Worth More*, we will explore how to change the meanings of these events if they shaped a low self-worth in you and how to forgive yourself and others for the wrongs you perceived that drained your self-worth battery gauge.

During early childhood, children develop a 'self-concept'. This is made up of the attributes, abilities, attitudes and values that they believe define them. Self-esteem can start as a baby, but develops progressively until the child has a more established sense of self-worth as early as five years old, according to the psychologist Dario Cvencek.

It can start in response to a child feeling safe, loved and accepted. As long-term memory develops, children also gain the 'remembered self'. This incorporates memories and information recounted by adults about events that form part of a person's life story. This is also referred to as 'autobiographical memory'. Young children develop an 'inner self', which is built on private thoughts, feelings, and desires that nobody else knows about unless a child chooses to let others know about these thoughts.

Your feelings of self-worth are built up very slowly, layer by layer, from a very young age, until they form a perceived reality construct. You take each meaning that you put on these events and people you interact with and make them your reality, which drives your self-worth. They are just then assumed to be true from then on, unless another significant event overwrites it, or you take on the responsibility of searching out those past meanings and changing the meaning in the interests of creating stronger self-worth. Most people simply don't know that they can do this, or don't have the tools to actually start unpicking the carbon-dated layers. I believe that your reality, in terms of both meanings you formed in the past and future perceptions, is fully malleable, and that, as a knock-on result, so is your self-worth.

Layer by layer and event by event we will explore how to work back to the origin of these self-worth-forming events and people, and gain a new perception of their meaning, to give you fresh, more balanced evidence and foundations to build your stronger sense of unshakeable self-esteem, value and confidence. No high fiving, clapping, dancing or hugging required. Maybe the odd 'fuck, yeah'.

8

The purpose of (low) self-worth

Self-worth can be defined as 'belief in one's own abilities'. Dictionary.com defines self-esteem as 'Confidence in one's own worth or abilities; self-respect'.

While you may not need a book to tell you that, something clearly defined is easier to measure and master. Later in *I'm Worth More* (Chapter 41) you will explore your non-negotiable code of conduct. Self-respect comes from maintaining your personal code of conduct, and not violating it. You will feel anger, frustration, guilt or shame, and perhaps even beat yourself into a pulp, if you violate your own values, ethics and moral code of conduct.

I could just say 'Don't do that', and then move swiftly on to the next point. But that's like saying to people struggling with money, 'Never spend more than you earn'. Logically, things are clear and easy. Emotionally and practically, they are often harder or more complicated.

When searching for definitions and reasons for the way things are, which I seem to do all the time, I find it important to also seek those reasons in reverse. The anti-reason, if you like. I was having a chat with my wife, who was quite shocked at the criticism and abuse she sees on Instagram. People taking pot shots at celebrities, or criticizing, bitching and pitching, blaming and complaining. She said, 'What is wrong with these people?'

Well, the reality I believe is 'nothing at all'. Why? Because we all complain about and criticize the people and things we stand against. When events and people oppose our values, we resist and fight them. And in so doing we become just as cruel or aggressive as the people we accuse.

All of us sometimes think 'Why don't we just be nice to everyone?' I think it often, too (mostly when people are criticizing me!), but denying ourselves the right to be critical of others would not ultimately serve our best interests. Nothing would get done. There would be no growth through challenge. There would be no evolution, and the survival of the species would be at risk. There would be nothing to stop us getting too powerful, selfish, greedy or lose touch with the principles of fair exchange. The critics serve to bring us back into balance. The support serves to lift us up and back into balance.

Any time we are out of that balance, at either extreme of having too much support or too much challenge, we will be offered feedback, events and solutions to bring us back into balance. It won't always be what you want, but it will always be what you need.

Think about it, have you ever been cruising and everything's going well and then, BANG, out of the blue you get blindsided? Something pretty bad happens. Just when things are starting to go well. Conversely, have you ever been really struggling, wondering when or even if things will get better, and then almost serendipitously something or someone comes along and gives you a break – a change or some support to lift you up?

I believe this seesaw, yin–yang balancing act exists in self-worth, too, because I believe it exists in everything. Your battery life is always charging up and draining out. Everything has an inherent and balanced upside and downside, a benefit and a drawback. People just fail to see the upside in the downside because they haven't cared to look closely enough. The upsides of high self-worth are evident, but high self-worth has equally balanced downsides, too:

- cockiness, arrogance or hubris
- lack of likeability and empathy
- driving big risks that backfire
- lack of self-awareness of your downsides
- lack of planning and preparation due to overconfidence
- learning and growth slowing or stopping due to you being a know-it-all
- ignoring criticism, warnings and useful feedback
- being chaotic and disruptive.

And, paradoxically, low self-worth has many (surprising) benefits:

- It can make you humble enough to want to learn and become a good student.
- It stops you making risky, reckless or life-threatening decisions and actions.
- It attracts teachers and supporters who lift you up.
- It creates low expectations which minimize failure and the 'comparison curse'.
- It can create modesty which is attractive to many people.
- It is likely to make you more open-minded towards others' points of view and advice.
- It focuses you on criticism and feedback, which in turn drives growth and improvement.
- It can motivate you to try to work harder and take less for granted.
- It can make you pessimistic and sceptical, which is a great skill in certain areas such as investing and quality control.

- It gives you an awareness of your limitations which can be better than overconfidence.

These are necessary and vital in many areas of your life, at different times. Low self-worth in the right areas for you – areas you have not yet recognized or mastered, or are low on your list of values – actually *serve* you. They stop you wiping yourself out like a lemming. They ensure perfect, harmonious balance of the species, allowing interdependence of serving and being served, under fair and equal exchange.

Taking it one step further, our self-worth *needs* to be low in the areas of non-value so we don't do things that others should be doing, or we shouldn't be doing. If you can see the gifts and the balance in the downsides in your low self-worth areas, then you can see them for the purpose that they serve you. You can then be grateful for them, not resentful of them and yourself. You can see that you need them. Knowing this can set you free.

On a more deep-rooted level, low self-worth actually plays an important part in our survival. The perception that we are not good or worthy is developed as a childhood defence against feelings of powerlessness and abandonment. Low self-worth is a way in which we try to cope with these emotions or events where we perceived we were neglected. Paradoxically, it gives us a feeling of control over events like parents separating, abuse, being sent away or a general lack of love. It eases our feelings of powerlessness. We tell ourselves it was our fault, that we are not worthy of love. This gives us the illusion of some control. We can then beat ourselves up about it, rather than punish others, which would increase the risk of retaliation and more abandonment and love withdrawal. The low self-worth acts as a defence mechanism. There's more on this later.

Moving through *I'm Worth More* I will not be suggesting that your entire life in all areas needs higher self-worth. In fact, many areas should stay as low as they are. My chronically low self-worth in the area of teaching yoga is perfect just as it is. The world does not need to see me in a leotard. Imagine a new-born baby giraffe trying to walk for the first time, with its gangly, wobbly legs, and you have the perfect vision of me adopting a yoga pose. My low self-worth in the area of being a surgeon is also perfect as it is. Don't give me a scalpel FFS.

When people tell you to work on all your weaknesses, be careful of this advice. Work on your weakest areas that affect your values and positive areas, such as people skills, sales or parenting. For everything else non-essential for your vision, leave it as it is. *Own* your low self-worth. Wear it like a badge of honour, because those areas make up the special, unique genius you are just as much as your skills and values.

9
Geography ... in French, of course

My reward for doing well in school, the year before my GCSEs, was to move up into the special top set in the year, where we were to learn a special new subject, Géographie. It even had an accent over the *e*. In this Géographie class, we were to be taught in and talk in only French.

For the last 25 years since then I have done so much with my French geography skills. Everywhere I go, real life, on the streets and in the markets, opportunities come up in business, parenting, relationships and money to implement and leverage the skills I learned and talents I developed in the classroom. Had it not been for this vital life-skill subject, I don't know how I would have survived in the tough dog-eat-dog world out there.

Not.

Sure, some subjects at school are useful and some necessary. It's not so much about what we *are* taught in most schools, but what we are *not* taught. We learn about strategies, but we don't learn about ourselves. We learn about what's outside, but not what's inside. Schools may be different now, but I was never taught how to understand the unique, complex, ever-so-slightly messed-up person that I am. I was never taught how to understand, manage and master my emotions. I was never taught about self-awareness, self-confidence or self-worth. And, boy, did I need them back then. Don't most youngsters and teenagers need that kind of education?

Don't most adults?

Ignorance is *not* bliss; it's ignorance. You don't know what you don't know. My previous self, who had no idea of the malleable nature of perception and reality, could have really done with some education in the area of general life skills.

This needs to be changed. How that is done on a local, national and global scale is for a different book at a different time. But for now, please do yourself and your children a favour and take on this responsibility yourself. Your education and reality are not fixed. Your upbringing and genetics do not have to define who you want to be.

There is a later chapter on self-awareness and knowledge. This must surely be the best investment in your personal development. Strategies and economies will come and go, but you will be with *you* your whole life. You're here, reading this, and that is a great place to start or to be. So thank you.

PART 2

(How) do you value yourself?
(All the things you say to yourself)

10
How you label yourself

What you say to yourself, and how you treat yourself, defines you. The world will do a good enough job of beating you up; there's no need to do it to yourself, too.

How you talk to, define and then 'label' yourself comes first from how other people of influence label you. Your parents, friendship circles, the (social) media, your teachers and other authority figures are all imposing their values, beliefs and labels on you. This is not a 'fault' of theirs, because this is what we *all* do. We push out and project on to others what we believe to be true. We react emotionally and 'lash out' at others in the moment. We transfer on to others our baggage of the past that arises in the present, triggered by a person or event. We try to convince people of our beliefs, and that they are the right and only beliefs to follow. We tell people what they can and can't do, and who they should and shouldn't be.

This serves us sometimes, and hinders us at others. Either way it is a reflection of other people's beliefs and experiences, not our own. When we are young or vulnerable, we need protection, and so helpful, experienced authority figures navigating us through a hard world can keep us safe.

A parent will try to protect their child, often by shielding them from the pain *they* experienced (way back in the past) as a child. Their father was hard on them, so they become soft. Their mother had so many rules, so they give more freedom. These projections are not better or worse, they are different.

We just perceive that they are better or worse based on our own (painful or significant) experiences.

Sometimes our friends and family will tell us a new business idea is risky. Or how we should or shouldn't raise our kids. Or that we shouldn't borrow money. Or that we have a safe job and a secure family, so we should just stick at it and be grateful. Stay in your lane. Sometimes, they are saying this *because* they care. They love us and want to protect us. But they are giving us advice based on *their* own experience and limited beliefs. Sometimes people tell us this because they tried and failed, or they don't want us to succeed, and they want to hold us back to make themselves feel better.

I have used the word 'sometimes' rather a lot here! But this is the point: sometimes it helps, sometimes it doesn't. Sometimes people care; other times they don't. The world is continually trying to influence us towards its belief system for its own motives. All of the current beliefs and labels you own and hold to be true have come from the external world. Most of them unconscious, unfiltered and as a by-product of your environment.

The first step in taking control of your self-worth is to be aware that this has happened and that it is totally normal. It's not good or bad, better or worse, lucky or not, it just *is*. It is who you are.

The second step is to start filtering, choosing, selecting and controlling what beliefs and labels you accept from the outside world about who you are, and what you choose to own and wear with pride, and what you choose to firmly reject.

Have you ever given yourself any of these labels?

- I'm a failure or loser.
- I'm a fraud.
- I'm a freak or weird.

- I was born unlucky.
- I'm too old, young, ugly, fat, short [insert your uniqueness].
- I'm average, nothing special.
- I'm stupid, thick, slow to learn.
- I always mess things up.
- Life's not fair for me.
- I'm not worth it.
- I'm not smart or good enough.
- I'm useless, helpless, hopeless.
- I'm not credible (no one will listen to me).

No. You are not any of these. Sure, you have *done* many of these. Once. Or many times. But not always. None of these are *who you are*, they are simply what you do or have done.

And then there's the big, overruling one:

- I can't do this.

Says who?

A critic? A 'friend'? Your family? An armchair expert?

Just because someone says it can't be done, doesn't mean you can't do it. What it usually means is *they don't know how*. Or *they* failed. Or *they* don't want you to succeed so you don't make them look bad.

Or, they care deeply.

I have a simple rule when it comes to advice. That could be family, friends, mentors, keyboard warriors, critics, haters, trolls or wankers. And the rule is this. It is simple. Follow this rule. It is an A or B choice:

- A If they are experienced, proven, qualified, and you respect them, then listen to them.
- B If they are not, then *don't*.

Be polite. Or firm. Or quiet. But, 100 per cent, *you* have to know how and what to select or reject what is right and wrong for *you*. Be choosy about what and who you decide to believe. Know when they are lashing out, or when they are caring (but inexperienced), or when the advice is warranted and qualified.

When *you* place those labels on yourself, you start to own the identities others have projected on to you. In some areas of your life, your labels are positive, empowering and confident. You are sure of yourself, and you label yourself like the star that you are. And before you go bashing the authority figures in your life that projected bad labels on to you, and go and bollock them for ruining your life, know that they also projected the good labels on to you.

But in many areas these labels can really hold you back and down. Labels become identities, and as such you exhibit behaviours associated with the label, even if those behaviours aren't really you, or don't really serve you, or aren't who you want to become. Your mind will hold on for dear life to the identities of who you are, because it is the very self-image and essence of your entire being; it is the order preventing the chaos.

Have the wisdom and self-authority, which is already in you, to pick and choose what you label yourself. Be kind to yourself when you are cruel to yourself, to balance your labelling. Pick yourself up when you put yourself down. Own your great traits as well as your flaws.

Labels imposed upon you by others (and yourself) are not just related to who you are, but where you are. These can be quite exaggerated and disempowering. Have you ever given yourself the following labels for a rut or road block you are facing?

- I've hit a brick wall.
- There's a huge weight on my shoulders.
- I'm drowning or sinking in [paperwork, shit, other].

It's funny (not funny) how we completely exaggerate the reality. And not even in a way that is fun or empowers us; rather in a way that totally debilitates us. I mean, if you hit a brick wall, that would really bloody hurt. What's the huge weight on your shoulders? An elephant? And can you imagine drowning in shit? No, don't. But people place those exaggerated labels on themselves when they are a bit overwhelmed or they have one small challenge.

Do yourself a huge favour and call yourself out each time you label yourself or a situation you feel you are in. Notice it, and then contextualize it. Remember the three As: Aware; Accept; Act. At least speak the truth to yourself. Your labels become the identity of who you are, so choose very carefully the labels you accept from others and place on yourself. That will become easier when you have a clear vision of who you are and who you want to become (we'll look at this in a later chapter).

11

Self-doubt

The purpose of self-doubt, like the purpose of low self-worth, is to stop you walking off the cliff to your imminent death like that lemming. Some things you absolutely *should* question, and doubt, and be sceptical about. Things you have never done before. Things that are risky or dangerous. Things that could ostracize you from your community. Things that are a threat to your survival.

The challenge comes when the self-doubt becomes debilitating, suffocating, or just plain inappropriate. When the self-doubt spills over from realistic, useful doubt, as when jumping out of an aircraft without a parachute, to misplaced, useless self-doubt such as public speaking to a small audience.

Once the doubt creeps into the realms of fantasy, once it takes power and control over you, the voices start. And they get louder and louder. And they take on a split personality. And they taunt you:

- It will all go wrong.
- I'm not good enough.
- They will laugh at me.
- My parents won't be proud of me.
- I will look like a fool.
- I'll never make it work.
- I don't deserve it.
- I won't live up to expectation.

- It's expensive, risky – what if I lose money?
- I never finish things.
- It's the wrong time.
- People will think I've changed.

These are all fantasies of your mind. These are you talking to yourself, or a parent or authority figure taunting you in your imagination. They are figments and warped memories of the past dragged up and taking the present out of context. They are only as real as you make them. Somewhere in the world, someone who has a less developed skillset in an area you are a legend at has more belief than you with less proof and reason to have it.

I have trained and helped a lot of people. Many, not all, go on to great things in a relatively short period of time, with little previous experience in the field. Once they get to a certain level of proficiency, the critics and haters usually appear out of their dark and dirty caves. If I had a UK pound (as long as it is strong against the dollar) for every time I heard a critic attack them, tell them that they know nothing, and point out that they (the critic) have 25 years' experience, then I'd be in the running to be the world's first trillionaire.

The reason the critic has become the critic, despite all the time, knowledge and experience they have, is nearly always down to the fears, doubts and low self-worth issues we've addressed so far in this book. Instead of leveraging all that experience, they have become side-tracked and defeatist, and turned their energy towards criticizing others as a way to feel better about themselves.

I understand and have sympathy for this. We've all felt like this. It's not a reflection of the protagonist, but a self-reflection of the voids, fears and labels of the critic. The critic can also be your inner voice; that can be worse than any outer critic could ever be. We will address that inner critic later in *I'm Worth More*, or the inner 'bas-tard', as I call it in *Start Now. Get Perfect Later*, as my inner voice really is a bas-tard.

The usual-suspect causes of self-doubt are twofold: practical and emotional. It is wise to know the difference. I am not a woo-woo huggy-happy-clappy high-five-brotha kind of person. Not all issues of self-doubt are because of emotional baggage we have carried since we were five years old. Some are simply practical. Others run deep. Here they are, broken into the two causes:

Practical:

- Too many opinions
- Too many options (leading to confusion and overwhelm)
- It's unproven (new)
- Wrong timing (real, not excuse)
- Lack of the required skills or resources
- People dragging you down
- A quandary or pull in different directions

Emotional:

- Past perceived failures
- Low general self-worth or belief
- Comparing ourselves to others
- Performance anxiety
- Fear of rejection and ridicule
- Being a perfectionist (never being or having enough, therefore never starting)
- Fear of success
- Believe what critics and others say about us

Some additional things you can do to manage and then master your self-doubt are:

- Do something small towards the bigger action.
- See your action as a test rather than final, unchangeable and absolute.
- List out as many pros and cons for the action and rule them out or in.
- Look to outsource it to someone else who is better at it.
- Ask for help and advice from mentors and smart counsel.
- Get 70 to 80 per cent of the research done, then do something (anything).
- Make a decision and make *that* right, rather than mulling over the right decision.
- Don't take yourself too seriously and enjoy yourself.
- Listen and read up on being decisive (it's like a muscle and can be strengthened).

Doubt can start as a wise apprehension at first, and quickly descend into more or all areas of your life and identity. Be wary of how it can snowball. Be mindful not to make one small thing mean all things, and take on the identity of always doubting yourself. Be aware of how you talk to yourself.

There's a small language, but huge actual, difference between your inner critic and inner critique. These will be addressed in the relevant chapters. But, for now, remember this:

There is no set benchmark for when you should or shouldn't start, or how good or ready or experienced you need to be. So, stop doubting and start shouting. Stop hiding and start grinding. Stop whining and start shining.

12

The comparison curse

Imagine if you had absolutely no one to compare yourself to. How would you feel about yourself if you didn't feel less worthy (or successful) than anyone else? If comparing wasn't a 'thing'? If you're going to compare yourself to anyone, compare yourself to where you were when you weren't as good or as far in as you are now. Maybe you'd compare yourself now to the lowest point in your life, to see just how far you've come. Maybe you'd compare yourself to the lowest point you possibly could be, the very worst it could ever be, so you felt better about where you are now, even if it isn't where you want to be.

Imagine if everyone was shit. Be honest, you'd probably secretly love it and feel instantly good about yourself. Even if you were nearly as shit.

No matter how good anyone else is, or how shit anyone else is, it changes absolutely nothing about *who you are*. You are you. Why should knowing how good or shit anyone else is change your self-image of how good you are, because it doesn't change the reality of who you are.

My writing this book does not make me any more knowledgeable on this subject matter. Other than perhaps how to write books – which is not the subject of this book! I know exactly the same about the content of this book whether I have written it for publication, or it is in a Word document, or it is in my head.

But the perception is that as a published author I know more about this subject because my knowledge is presented in the form of a book. Someone else, yet to write a book (or never likely to) could well know more, but never write it down. Then, if I make no sales of my book, I will feel less worthy, despite what I know, and who I am, not changing at all. If the books fly off the shelf, I will feel better and more worthy, despite what I know and who I am not changing at all.

Comparison has useful benefits, but often becomes a 'curse' because we tend to focus on the negative. We tend to focus on what we haven't got compared to others, where we haven't got to compared to others and who we are not compared to others. That makes us feel worse than who we actually are, because it changes the context. But it doesn't change the reality of who we are, just like a book doesn't change what I know.

We compare ourselves to others for the following reasons:

- It is an external measure of value that gives context.
- It helps us survive and adapt in an ecosystem.
- It is a benchmark to drive growth and progress.
- It is a way of avoiding trailblazing and reducing risk through social proof.
- It is a valuable feedback mechanism.
- There is no other objective or universal benchmark to measure against.
- To feed an innate desire to assess skills and abilities, and for validation.
- To fuel feelings and voids of self-esteem and worth.

So, like all 'negative emotions', the comparison curse has its functions, and only becomes a curse when perceived from a one-sided, imbalanced perspective.

We can be sadomasochistic with the 'Comparison Curse'. It's like watching someone throw up. We know they are about to throw up. The last thing we want to do is watch someone throw up. But then we just have to watch them throw up. Then we are disgusted watching them throw up. Then we go and tell everyone how disgusting it was watching them throwing up. And in graphic detail, too. We both want to and don't want to compare ourselves to others. We know the disempowering path it can take us down, but we go down it anyway.

Comparison vis-à-vis others can happen in the following ways:

1 Upward comparison (someone you perceive as better) to:
   a inspire and motivate you to want more and be
      better
   b feel less worthy or able.

2 Downward comparison (someone you perceive as worse) to:
   a aggrandize yourself to feel superior or belittling
   b feel grateful and good about yourself.

Balancing these ways of using comparison in a more positive and productive way will stop you feeling less worthy than you really are. Some people say this can be achieved by not trying, or reducing your expectations, but I think there are more inspired and progressive ways to turn the comparison curse into a gift. This will be covered in Chapter 30 (Reverse comparison) as well as elsewhere in this book.

13

Beating yourself up

The world will do a good job of beating you up, so don't do it to yourself. There are enough critics out there without you being the harshest critic of all.

Of course, if it were this easy, you'd just stop beating yourself up. Instead, you beat yourself up about beating yourself up. You feel bad for feeling bad, only to feel even worse. And then you go and beat yourself up about that. And then you beat yourself up about everything else while you're at it.

I found that even with 12 years and more than £1 million invested in my personal development, in the form of books, podcasts, masterminds, mentorships and retreats, that, if I made a mistake, I'd beat myself up because I should know better. After all, I've done all this personal development. What a loser for doing all these courses and supposedly knowing myself, and then cocking up when I should know better, and I know what to do but I'm not doing it. Dickhead! (Me, not you.)

Like all these self-worth piranhas, there is a function and purpose behind them that brings balance and context to the extreme emotion you are feeling. The purposes of beating yourself up – yes, it does in fact have purposes – are:

- It helps you avoid making the same mistake over and over again.
- You need to feel increasingly worse about increasingly bad situations, so that you continually seek solutions, growth and progress.

- Because you have not yet learned to forgive or ask for forgiveness (others and self).

Beating yourself up serves to get you to lift yourself up. To step up. The more you beat yourself up, the more you need to step up, because the pain feedback is equal to the scale of the problem. Instead of beating yourself up for beating yourself up, beat yourself up quickly, have a hard word with your temporary loser self, a quick back-hand slap to the face, and then turn that inward energy outward to proactively take decisive actions to solve the challenges. The rewards at the end are the positive emotions you feel, and the bigger the challenge, the bigger the positive emotional reward.

The two main emotions we feel when beating ourselves up, or doubting ourselves, and often when comparing ourselves to others, are guilt and shame. These are similar emotions that we can confuse. They both underpin self-feedback and correction. Guilt appears when we think that we have done damage to something or someone. Shame appears when we believe that we are unworthy or damaged, unlovable, inferior or incompetent. The function, like beating yourself up, is self-feedback to correct personal moral and ethical codes and standards we live by that define our identity.

Guilt and shame are fear-based responses, and have differing levels of extremism. According to the health psychologist Kelly McGonigal, our brain has more fear responses than just the well-known fight or flight. If we believe we can manage the difficulty that we face, our brains are more likely to react with a 'challenge response'. Like other fear responses, the challenge response releases stress hormones (cortisol and adrenaline) in order to get us going. But it also releases oxytocin, which soothes us and motivates us to connect with others, and DHEA, which helps the brain learn from the situation.

This is productive stress. A forward-moving, action- and solution-oriented stress. This is the state in which you roll your sleeves up, take no shit and just get it done. You have the balanced reward emotion mixed in with stress hormones, to draw you towards the solution. If you have to beat yourself up, make it productive. It consumes a lot of energy to slap yourself around and talk shit to yourself. Turn that guilt and shame and stress and cycle of self-punishment 180 degrees, and hone that energy into something productive, such as one of the following:

- Smash a punch bag, kick some pads, pump some weights.
- Immediately go and help someone else, and convert the energy into something positive.
- Create a piece of content from what you learned bullying yourself.
- Journal or vlog or podcast on the subject.
- Have someone you trust who you can verbally throw up all over.
- Design, create, invent, build or make something; convert the energy into something productive/creative.
- Draw up a grand masterplan.

It's far better to take these proactive steps, even if somewhat haphazardly, than to fester and beat down on yourself. Un-released shame and excessive guilt can result in habitual self-analysis and self-condemnation, which can lead to depression, anxiety, resentment or anger issues. When we fail to deal with the stress emotions, or build them up inside ourselves, it further adds to the evidence that supports our negative self-beliefs. A 'shame cycle' begins in which we engage in and repeat destructive behaviours because we don't believe that we have the ability to change. We turn to temporary relief highs and addictions to block out the overwhelming feelings. The cycle continues after the comedown.

As children, we tell ourselves it must be our fault when things go wrong; that our parents don't love us the way we need them to. We convince ourselves that we had control over their love for us, and we can take it out on and punish ourselves, because it is easier and safer than punishing others. If we were to express our emotions, we may fear retaliation and rejection. We may push love and acceptance away. In the absence of someone else to punish us, we beat ourselves up so we can love ourselves again after a mistake.

I believe it is possible to turn all shameful and distressing situations into this 'positive stress' or 'challenge response'. You simply redirect the energy from inward to outward. From negative into positive. When I say 'simply', I mean simple, but not easy. You know the things you love to do, make, create, build, analyse and immerse yourself in. I used throwing myself into my start-up business to help me through loneliness. I use my podcast and social media as a channel to vent and rant about the things that the world throws at me every day and express the emotions I would otherwise repress. All this will be explored further in Part 5.

14
Fear of success(!)

This seems as strange to many as it is normal to some. The paradox of success is that, once achieved, there is a certain level of expectation to be lived up to. Many people fear how people will perceive them once they are successful, as if they have changed or have forgotten where they came from and now feel superior. People may fear criticism or ridicule, or that they are an impostor. This could make you feel like an outcast from your normal environment and friendship circles. Many people feel they want to fit in, and success can make you stand out.

We can have fear-based emotions linked to success. Like the fear of taking risks or, worse, failure. After all, the more successful we become, the bigger the potential failure. The bigger the public humiliation potential. The more there could be to lose. The bigger sacrifices that need to be made. The more responsibility there is to uphold. The more people will demand of you. Could you handle all that expectation?

Once you are successful, there is nowhere else to go. Nothing else to achieve. That is scary for some. Maybe the view from the top of the mountain will not be what you dreamed of for so long? Or there may be huge pressure to stay there and be at the top. Others may fight you to oust you from being number one. If we don't get there, we don't have to live up to anything or anyone. We don't have to face the fact that there is no 'happy ever after' or state of perfect perennial success. A 'normal' life is easy and comfortable. Success is complicated and uncomfortable and even terrifying.

Some people simply feel they don't deserve it and couldn't handle it.

On a practical level, success can make demands on your time or changes to your routine that might be inconvenient. It might take you away from friends, family, hobbies, health and fitness.

Success means being in a new environment. Like animals, people fear being in a new environment because of the risks and threats to their safety. This serves a good purpose and is absolutely normal. It is a self-defence mechanism that stops us from going into the unknown. You should have a well-managed, balanced fear regarding new environments.

One of the biggest fears can be that we will become unlovable once successful. Many of the combined fears of judgement, change and expectation all link to the fear of how others judge, ridicule or don't love you. And that is one of our deepest fears, and, as such, there can be a lot of pain attached to the pursuit of success. For some people, it is a result of emotional trauma growing up, or from their parents or an authority figure. Examples could be a woman who is afraid to be more successful than her husband, or a woman who is afraid to be more successful than her mother, where they feel the penalty could be a withdrawal of love or acceptance. There's more on this later.

The irony in the fear of success is that it often paralyses us and stops us acting when the future that we fear is so far away and there are so many steps to take before we actually get there. At least give yourself a chance to taste a small amount of success for yourself, as a little test, to get the proof of what it is really like, before you write it off completely.

The reality of the success you seek will be different from how you perceive it anyway, so let the reality play out as it will. Things you imagine will be hard, won't. Things you perceive will be easy, won't. Things you plan for won't matter. Things you don't plan for will appear or catch you out. Be mindful when you are only perceiving the downside of success, and look to balance it out.

Sure, there are costs to success. There are sacrifices. No doubt about it. But what are the costs and sacrifices of staying where you are? You may well miss out on:

- all the money you want and more
- all the freedom, choice and autonomy
- all the praise, adulation and love from your fans, followers and customers
- all the kindness and money and time you can give to your family, others and yourself
- becoming the best version of yourself
- worldly adventures, travel and luxury
- great people, contacts and network
- time for family, friends, hobbies
- working not because you have to but because you want to
- increased self-worth
- a more attractive, radiant, compelling and charismatic you.

So, what price do *you* want to pay? What sacrifice do you want to make?

Judge what success is really like when you get there, FFS!

And when people say 'You've changed'? Well, *of course* you've changed. Who wants to be (known as) the same person as they were ten years ago? Your values, morals and ethics can be the same, but all else about you can be better.

And for every person that will 'hate about you the very thing that is great about you', others will love everything about you. They will admire and respect you. You will be the light that inspires them to a better life. And that is one of the best feelings there is.

And if you find, when you reach the dizzy heights of success, that you hate it and don't want any of it, no problem at all, just give it to me and I will take care of it for you!

15
Living up to expectations of you

The expectations of others, especially parents and influential authority figures, can add a whole heap of pressure to live up to. Often, who you feel you need to live up to is not who you are, and that can compound the pressure and resultant anxiety and inner conflict.

I was overweight as a kid. No, I was fat. In fact, I was the token fat kid in my school. If I had been the second fattest kid, I'd have had somewhere (or someone) to hide behind. But no. I was the fattest kid. It was shit. I still carry some baggage from when I was 12 with me more than 25 years later, but to keep this relevant, I wanted to make my dad proud. My dad loves rugby and really wanted me to play.

So, I played rugby. I was prop, of course, because that's where the fat kids play. Every new season the kit would be distributed and even the largest size would be way too small on me. I would wrestle to put it on – it was like trying to get in and out of a straitjacket for a magic show. There was no stretch in clothes back then, and the lower half of my belly hung out of the bottom.

I was maybe the second or third slowest sprinter in the whole year. Each time we had athletics I would sprint hard while all the other kids watched and sniggered as my man-tits wobbled all over the place and I looked like I was trying to wade through treacle to the finish line. It would take me about an hour and a half to do the 100 metres.

My dad would come to every rugby game. I loved him being there. The other kids loved him. He used to get really involved in the games, team talks, and some of the training. Not like those really annoying dads who start fights and rant expletives, but someone helpful and motivating – it made me proud to be his son.

But I fucking hated rugby. I hated the shame of my belly and my man-tits. I hated the fact that I couldn't run though I tried so damn hard. I hated the cold and the wet. I hated hugging other men and having the lock behind me grab my balls in the scrum. And, worst of all, I hated what the other kids jeeringly said about me. I was mostly the butt of all the fat jokes, and when I wasn't I thought I was because I had become so paranoid about it.

I played rugby for three seasons and hated every single minute of it, except the rare occasion when I scored a try, usually when the ball was passed to me a few yards from the try line and I would mow down about 15 skinny kids (and the referee) thanks to my tank-like momentum. I would fear the rugby season at least one term before it came around, which part-ruined one-third of my school year.

I played rugby only because I wanted to live up to who my dad wanted me to be. I thought that my dad watching me play rugby was an expression of love and I wanted him to be proud of me. Unlike some parents, he put no pressure on me to do it – he just assumed I would – and it was never discussed because that's not how it was back then. In fact, sharing this story here might be the first time I've ever shared it fully.

I put myself through all that pain, never questioning any choice I had in it, to live up to my dad's expectation and to get his love. But I know for a fact that he loves me anyway, and would love me whether I played rugby or not. I never understood this. I felt I had to do what he wanted me to, to be good enough in his eyes.

It was a hard lesson that took me more than 20 years to learn. You do not have to live up to anyone's expectation of you. If they love you, they will love you no matter who you are, for who you are, and no matter what you do, as long as it is legal and ethical. Even if it isn't, we all make mistakes and they will likely forgive you.

It is common for us to seek the love and approval of others, because as human beings we need love. It is one of our evolutionary advantages, but it also causes conflicting feelings of conditional love, the pressure of letting people down and a need for wanting people to love or approve of us and our actions. The fear of not receiving love, as in the fear of success or comparing ourselves to others, is so strong sometimes that we will self-sabotage. Or play a sport for three years that you loathe and in clothes way too tight for you.

You are your own person who doesn't have to live up to any expectation of you. As long as you are living according to your values, and doing morally positive things, then be grateful for those who admire, love and respect you, and accept, or even be grateful for, those who stand against you. You do not need their approval; you need your own. You need your love, not the love of other people.

There are some balanced upsides to the need for approval, and it can be productive and positive to get the love of those close to you. This will be discussed in Chapter 24 (The need for approval).

16

The perfectionist paradox

Perfectionism is often worn as a badge of honour, like it's a trait of greatness. As though anyone or anything that isn't perfect is a failure.

In a job interview, one of the most common answers I hear to the 'areas of weakness' question is 'I'm a perfectionist'. The interviewee then proceeds to spin it into a strength: 'But that makes me soooo great at my job.' Then you hire them. Then six months later they leave because their brain melted out of their ears and they couldn't handle anything being out of place. Screw you for moving one of their ducks.

The pressure of expectation, fear of failing, comparison, social media filtering, Photoshop, cosmetics and hyped-up success stories all add to the weight of the perfectionism curse. The paradox in perfectionism is that the greater the expectation of perfectionism, the more imperfect the reality is perceived to be. The greater the distance (or void) between the height of absolute perfection and the cold reality, the greater the stress. In extreme cases, this turns to obsessive compulsive disorders that can spill over into personality disorders, eating disorders, social anxiety, workaholism, substance abuse, self-harm and clinical depression.

If you feel you have an extreme case like this, please seek professional help. If you can see yourself going down that road, this book should help you take control back. I can put huge pressure on myself to live up to ridiculous expectations, and have certainly experienced the pain of perfectionism. It's no fun at all, and it's mostly self-inflicted.

I often find myself superstitious. My inner voice (bas-tard) taunts me to go back home to check I haven't left lights on, 'touch wood' and do things in very specific orders. It could be making the bed a specific way, or spending ages tidying and organizing before doing anything, not stepping on cracks on the pavement or taking the exact same route to the train station. It could be more extreme: Howard Hughes-style cleanliness and washing your hands so many times. A classic is how you hang up pictures or order things in the house or the colour-coordinating your wardrobe. My inner bas-tard even says things like 'If you don't go back and close the door, your son will be kidnapped.'

We beat ourselves up on every small defect. Tiny little things that wouldn't bother many other people. Tiny things that others don't even notice or make any real difference. Tiny things that are out of our control. We get superstitious. We fear failure, ridicule or judgement. It builds and becomes obsessive. We feel the need to control everything.

Little by little, we belittle ourselves and erode our peace of mind. We criticize ourselves for every perceived tiny flaw, failing or under-achievement. We think: had I only done this or had I only *not* done that, then the outcome would have been perfect.

But it never is.

The paradox of perfectionism is that we are perfectly imperfect. We are perfect just as we are. We are not broken. We are flawed and unique, and we make mistakes. We need to strive for better to grow, to learn and to fight off boredom and atrophy. A need for perfectionism can drive progress and constant improvement. But let it get the better of you, and it soon becomes a curse that controls you.

Sometimes less or even no expectation is better than the pain of perfectionism. That doesn't mean not trying hard; it just means shortening the gap between expectation and reality. If you expected to die tomorrow, every day you wake up would be a great gift. You would live life only for the things that mattered the most.

Only control what you can. Learn to let go of what you can't. Trying to control external factors, outcomes and people will compound the pain of perfectionism. At least when it is you, you can do something about it. But to try to control things over which you have no control is a sure-fire way to feel, at best, bad and, at worst, at dis-ease.

The more perfect you need something to be at the end, or before you start, the harder it is to start. Perfectionism is a curse of progress. Strive for professional and personal excellence, not perfection. 'Start now. Get perfect later', as I've said before!

I edited and edited and edited and edited my book *Money*. It took me months and months. I thought I would be happier with each edit, expecting improvements each time. But, with each edit, when I was supposed to reduce word count, I would edit out 5,000 words but write in 5,000 words. Five edits, and the book was still 70,000 words over the amount my publisher was expecting. It was tying my mind in knots. In the end, I just had to let it go. Thank goodness for the publishing deadline or I might still be editing it at my funeral. The publisher has great copyeditors. I'd done my bit. I'd done more than enough. It was time to let it go. I found it hard at first, but now it is easier. I will now do two edits, get a group of critics to edit one last time, and then the book is sent to the publisher and I let it go.

If I can learn to do this, I can apply it in other areas of my life where I am a control freak and never satisfied. You get to a point with perfectionism where things aren't actually getting better. They are just getting different. Or worse. And you are making it that way. I've been tweaking my latest hi-fi upgrades. It is a perfectionist's paradise. I demo'd speaker after speaker after speaker. I nearly bought a pair of £53,000 speakers without listening to them, assuming they would be musical perfection. After going around the houses, the pair I already had ended up being the best. Don't get into diminishing returns or paranoid perfectionism.

Perfect would be boring anyway. You'd lose purpose. You'd have nowhere else to go and to grow. People are attracted to your flaws (OK, not all of them!). No one relates to perfection; they relate to (real) people.

17
Warning: what you do isn't who you are

Some people attach most or all of their self-worth to one thing they do. That could be their job, being a parent, a single talent or skill, or making people laugh. It could be your business, your knowledge or your standing in society.

Attaching all your self-worth to one (external) thing is very risky to your self-worth, because, if that one thing fails, *you* fail. If you lose that one thing, you can lose not just that one thing, but your entire sense of who you are – everything. You make *yourself* insignificant, a failure and not worthy, because without that one thing, you have nothing.

When your kids leave home or your business goes under, or you get fired or retire, or your talent goes because you get old or injured or obsolete, what next? What you do isn't left; all that is left is you: who you are. You're magnificent and full of infinite potential, as long as you separate your self-worth from your one (or many) things that you do.

What you do is a single action, or a series of actions, that results in a single skill or outcome. This is one action or skill out of an infinite number of things that make up the identity and being of who you are. What you do, well or badly, doesn't define you.

Stephen King's first book, *Carrie*, was rejected by 30 publishers. Walt Disney was fired from his newspaper job because he 'lacked imagination and good ideas'. Oprah Winfrey was fired from her first TV job because someone thought she was 'unfit for TV'. Winston Churchill failed sixth grade and was considered 'a dolt' by his teacher. Jerry Seinfeld was booed off the stage the first time he tried comedy.

You are not one mistake. You just made one mistake. You are not one failure. You just failed once. Or sometimes. Or even lots. Conversely, you are not one success. You just succeeded once. You will know the feeling if you ever got cocky and fell from grace.

'I did shit' is a million miles away from 'I am shit'. Keep it that far apart. Do not 'personalize' any failure. In the modern age, with people living decades longer than 100 years ago, and with access to information faster than ever, you can reinvent yourself many times over. Gone are the days where you were destined for one career your whole life.

Players can become coaches, kids can become social-media celebrities, students can become teachers, politicians can become keynote speakers – the options and abilities to change career are bigger and better than ever before. You can even use the life-disrupting event as a lesson, even an opportunity. Stevie Wonder was blind. Beethoven wrote some of his best work after he'd gone deaf. Dave Mustaine co-formed Megadeth after being kicked out of Metallica.

In fact, more and more people are embracing this flexibility to change professions. People are intentionally changing their careers, lifestyles and locations frequently. They desire not to be bound or defined by any label or position. I mean Arnie made it big in three separate, unrelated careers. Harrison Ford was a car-penter for 15 years before he was an actor. Mickey Rourke was a professional boxer before an injury forced his retirement. John Grisham was a lawyer for a decade before he became a writer.

Nature abhors a vacuum. Where one door closes another door opens. (Insert other clichés about opportunity here.) You have infinite, intrinsic value. What you lose you can get back. What you lose for ever you can do without. *You* aren't any less. What you *do* is never who *you* are.

18
If you don't value yourself ...

... then why should anyone else? If you don't believe in yourself, then why should anyone else?

Imagine going to a job interview and saying 'Hi, I'm Dave, and I have no value at all. I'm useless and worthless. Got any vacancies?' Imagine pitching for money to someone and saying, 'Hi, I'm Tracy, I don't value myself at all but will you lend me some money?'

You probably know someone who knows less than you in an area you know well. It could be a passion or profession of yours. It could be a competitor. That someone probably has a bit about them, maybe they're bold, cocky and happy to 'fake it 'till they make it'. While these people don't always have enduring success, they can get a fast start. You might perceive them as a bullshitter, and their blagging might really get under your skin. However, if you are really honest, there are things about them you admire, things you would secretly love to have and things you can learn from.

If you were lending *your* hard-earned money, would you rather lend it to someone who believes in themselves, even if they are a little cocky, even if they haven't got years of credibility to back it up, or someone who has no belief, confidence in and value of themselves?

To value yourself is not to be arrogant or narcissistic. It is to know your worth and value. To know your traits and skills. To own them. To show the world confidently that you've got this.

That you are worth this. That you can take on responsibility. That you can solve problems. And to be able to give it to the world (which the world needs) you need to give it to yourself first.

In my book *Life Leverage* I shared this story about Picasso that I wish I'd known when I lacked confidence and self-worth:

Picasso, the story goes, was sitting in a Paris café when an admirer approached and asked if he would do a quick sketch on a paper napkin. Picasso politely agreed, swiftly executed the work, and handed back the napkin, but not before asking for a rather significant amount of money. The admirer was shocked, 'How can you ask for so much? It took you a minute to draw this!'

'No,' Picasso replied, 'It took me 40 years!'

And so it is with you. You have lived your whole life becoming a unique person with a unique make-up of skills and talents and experiences. That includes the great traits as well as the voids and weaknesses that act as a balancing force.

Others are honouring, owning, packaging and selling their life's work and value, so why can't you? We all buy into a compelling story and are inspired by the lives of others. So make sure that you are telling the world your story. The story of your whole life that fills you with worth, experience and wisdom that can inspire, serve and add value to others' lives, too.

On a deeper level, if you don't love yourself, then it will be hard for others to love you. I'm not talking hippy-happy-clappy love, but true-to-*you* self-love. You can't give what you don't have, so to get more worth and love, rather than seeking it externally, you need to fill yourself with it first. There's more on the subject of (self-)love in Part 3.

On a financial level, if you don't value yourself, you won't value what you bring to your business or career. You won't value your time and you won't reflect that self-worth into fair high prices. You will overwork, undercharge and not attract the right quality of client, boss or company. You will be a poor receiver of money because you won't feel worthy of it. More on the subject of your self-worth and value around money in Part 6.

We beat ourselves up, we put ourselves down and we don't own our own value. After all, how many times do you actually list all the great things about you? For every one thought you have that knocks you down a little, do you immediately point out at least one great trait in you? Many people have spent much time internally going over all the things they did wrong and the mistakes and bad traits, but how many times have you sat down and made a list of 50 or 100 things about you that are great?

This isn't a workbook, but that wouldn't be a bad exercise to do for yourself, would it? What if you did it every week, or every time you were hard on yourself? How might that affect your perception of yourself?

And while we're at it. We often catch ourselves messing up. Bad parents, bad bosses, bad managers of money. Bad friends, bad partners, bad people. But how many times do you catch yourself out doing something well? How many times did you stop and pat yourself on the back for a small thing or a big thing that you nailed? 'Rob, you were a Casanova last night in the bedroom' (if last night was in 1995). Many people hardly ever give themselves credit.

If you are a parent, every day you don't shout at your kids is a great day and you deserve a 'parent of the year' medal of honour. If you run a business, every year you are still solvent you are *way* beating the odds and you should turn your staff party into a mass orgy. (Just wait for the complaints and one star reviews about my crass analogies, but I have great self-worth around them, ha!).

Life can be hard, and a lot of stuff you take for granted you are actually doing great at. You should be owning that. Value yourself, and the world will value you, because the world is a mirror of you and your perception. Imagine that, instead of beating yourself up, you lifted yourself up. Imagine that, instead of being your harshest critic, you were your biggest fan. Well, that's coming in Part 4.

19
They've labelled it 'impostor syndrome'

Do you ever feel like a fraud? Or that you are going to be 'found out'? That you don't deserve it? That you will inevitably lose it all? That you are not good enough to maintain your current, or any lasting, success?

Do you ever feel that you'd better get out or give up, because it will all fall apart soon enough? No matter how well you do, it's never good enough and you can't own your success. You often give up at things you are good at so you don't have to live up to the pressure and expectation. You self-sabotage as your own insurance policy against failure.

So they have a label for all that, and it has become a 'thing'.

'Impostor syndrome' (also known as impostor phenomenon, impostorism, fraud syndrome or the impostor experience) is a psychological complex in which an individual doubts their accomplishments and has a persistent internalized fear of being exposed as a 'fraud'. Despite external evidence of their competence, those experiencing this phenomenon remain convinced that they are frauds, and do not deserve all they have achieved.

People often feel like an 'impostor' and unfairly attribute their success to luck, or as a result of tricking others into thinking they are more intelligent than they perceive themselves to be. It's interesting that this is not a mental disorder but almost has a label that sounds like it is.

The causes of this feeling include:

- lack of positive feedback about you or your work
- low self-esteem and confidence
- strong fear of failure, despite (m)any achievements
- feelings of inadequacy
- perfectionism paradox, where a desire for perfection leaves us dissatisfied with our actions or paralysed into inaction.
- high self-importance or unrealistic expectations that set up feelings of failure
- intellectual fraudulence (some actually do exaggerate so the fear of being found out is real)
- potential for public criticism, punishment or shame for making mistakes
- conditional worth or love, only gained through high achievement or success.

When I started investing in property, we had about five minutes to enjoy it, and then the epic recession of 2008 came. We saw investors and companies around us drop like flies. We were young and lean (in terms of overheads, not the six-pack kind), and although it was hard at times, it didn't affect us anywhere nearly as badly as all the bigger players. We were one of the few companies left, and became relevant almost by default. The upside was that we learned a lot from those who struggled, we kept overheads low and stashed money away. But it did create some fears in us. Fears that it could happen to us next time, that we were lucky this time and that we didn't deserve and hadn't earned our elevated position.

It's funny how we manage to find a downside to everything. These 'impostor' emotions served to keep us humble and hungry, and to remind us to plan well for future challenges and disruptions. To further deal with and defeat your impostor feelings, try the following:

- Manage your self-importance and expectations so that they are better balanced or more realistic.
- Focus on giving value and helping others as a way to feel validated and worthy.
- Make a list of 50–100 great things about you and why you deserve success.
- Stop comparing yourself to others in an unbalanced manner.
- See all pursuits and successes as progressive tests rather than final destinations.
- Know that nothing you do or do not achieve defines who you are.
- The world needs your skills and talents so don't deny people them by self-sabotaging.
- Get clear on your vision and legacy and how you want to be remembered
- If impostor syndrome gets loud, write it all down as personal therapy. This really helps you to sleep, too, if it taunts you at night.
- Know that nobody knows what you are thinking, feeling and fearing inside.
- Practise owning, thanking and being grateful for your victories, successes and compliments. Celebrate them!
- Ask for help and share your feelings with professionals, friends, advisors and mentors.
- Know that we are all struggling with self-worth, even your idols and huge celebrities

If you have these impostor emotions, naming them as external 'things' can compartmentalize them, and banish them as literal impostors that don't have a space in your head. But beware of labelling them so much, however, that you give them an identity and start to take ownership of them. People can use labels as excuses and validations, which is not productive.

Each time a fear of being found out rears its butt-ugly head, think of all the things you will gain the more successful you are, and all the things you will lose by letting the impostor talk you out of your goals and self-worth.

20

Every winner was once a beginner

Or to put it another way: every master was once a disaster.

When you compare yourself to others, or idolize your heroes, or doubt your abilities relative to the success of the greats, or when you label yourself, beat yourself up and don't value yourself, it is easy to forget that everyone was once a beginner. There was a day when even your idol had no experience, no idea and were further back than you are now.

We all start somewhere, even the greats who make it look graceful and effortless. It often took them decades of hard work to make it look that easy. No one was born the finished genius that they are; they were simply born with the infinite potential to become that. Tiger Woods didn't pop out of his mum and boom a 300-yard drive. Until scientists find exact chromosomes for 'World number 1 golfer', I am never going to believe that anyone is genetically born with predetermined skills or vocation.

Skills and vocations are learned and developed over many years of purposeful practice, smart-hard work, experience, coaches and mentors, mistakes and failures, and constant feedback and improvement.

There are, of course, physical and biological restraints, such as the 5-foot basketball player who couldn't slam-dunk or a one-armed golfer who couldn't compete at the highest level ... But wait a moment ...

Tyrone 'Muggsy' Bogues was the shortest player ever to play in the National Basketball Association. At 5 foot 3 inches,

Bogues played point guard for four teams during his 14-season career in the NBA including ten seasons with the Charlotte Hornets. He scored 24 points in a game three times, not bad for someone supposedly not tall enough to play basketball.

One close to my heart is Tommy Morrissey, who is the same age as my son, and a fellow talented golfer. Tommy came fourth in the US Kids World Golf Championships. One difference between him and the other kids in the tournament is that he was born with one arm, and swings the club with his left arm only.

So even with severe physical restrictions, it is possible to become anything you want to be, as long as it is humanly possible. No one who is where you want to be in life, business or net worth, owns all of it. Nobody with skills and traits you admire as a person, like charisma, was born with them. No one is doing something you couldn't do, with the right mix of persistence and prolonged purposeful practice.

Even in extreme cases where it isn't physically possible for you to be a great, you can get close, or you can do something similar. Someone who desired to be a professional golfer could become a great coach or course designer. Someone who wanted to be a musician could be a great producer or agent.

Instead of comparing yourself to where the masters and greats are now, or the pinnacles they reached, you could compare yourself to where they were at the stage that you are at now. They were likely just where you are, or even further back. At exactly the time I am writing this sentence Alistair Cook has just finished his record-breaking career in English cricket. He has broken virtually every record: number of total runs for an English player, any left hander in the word, all openers in the world, fifth in the all-time runs list.

It is widely accepted that Cook was not the most talented. His technique was limited and in some cases flawed, and he didn't have the range of shots of some other greats. But Cook worked within his set of skills, was very clear who he was, and became the very best that he could be. Cook is a great example of your everyday hero. Of course, most people who play cricket will never be like Cook, but there will be many more 'talented' players who will not reach his heights.

You could also compare yourself to where you were when you first started. Even one grade up in martial arts is better than white belt. In the martial arts classes I went to as a boy, if you had done three or four gradings, you were allowed to pair up and teach the white belts some moves, even if you'd only been training a few months. You can often surprise yourself by how far you've come, if you take the time to look back.

You can take an area you are skilled in, you have achieved and excelled in, and transmute some of that experience and knowledge into your new area. Or, better, your entire self-worth. You may be a great parent but just starting a part-time business. What can you learn from the greatness already in you, and leverage it into a new vocation or skill? Of course, it is smart to model the traits of the greats, but you can literally model yourself. This is great for your self-worth all round.

And, finally, don't spend all your time wishing you were great and experienced, and therefore forget to enjoy where you are at now. We can spend so much of our time looking to the future that we forget to breathe in the present moment. We literally miss the gifts right in front of our face. I recall starting my first company, Progressive Property, in January 2007. I so badly wanted to be successful, and have hundreds of properties, and be a multimillionaire, that for three years at least I never really allowed myself to be fully present in the start-up phase. I was always wanting more, and never happy with where we were at.

While that was good for drive and progress, it wasn't until I looked back with nostalgia that I realized that when we were just starting out:

- We had virtually no overheads and were lean.
- We could make a decision and implement it that day (not next tax year!).
- It was so exciting to dream big.
- We hadn't had any of the challenges yet and were blissfully naive.
- My business partner and I were both single, went out a lot and had some great times.
- Having no staff meant no responsibilities and more freedom.
- There was no VAT to start with and so there were higher profit margins
- We were so hungry to learn and prove ourselves.
- We had less fear.

If you look closely enough, you can see all the upsides of not being the finished article yet, or as far ahead as the masters. We are all made of the same stuff: we have limitless potential to be anything we want to be, as long as it is humanly possible. Every winner was once a beginner, and every master was once a disaster.

21
Your life's work (is who you are)

The story about Picasso, I hope, illustrates that it is your whole life that makes up who you are, how you value yourself, what you charge and how you show up in the world. Picasso's fees and self-worth were not in a five-minute sketch and signature on a napkin, but everything he had learned, experienced and created his entire life. Because value and worth are intangible and harder to universally benchmark, how you value yourself is the only absolute measure of your worth, which reflects outwards to your prices, salary and earning capacity.

You have lived your whole life becoming the unique person you are, with a unique make-up of skills and talents and experiences. You have lived through highs and lows. You have overcome challenges. You have made a difference in people's lives. You have made many mistakes and learned from them. You have read and studied, travelled and listened. You have a unique, valuable, transferrable perspective. Don't forget that. Or, rather, make sure that you remember and bring that into your ventures and endeavours.

Sometimes people say to me that there are a lot of 'influencers' and 'entrepreneurs' out there on social media saying much the same as me. They ask me how I perceive myself as different. How do they get into this space when there are so many out there already? Well, there is only one answer, and that is that they are not me, and I am me. They are not you, you are you. Sure, some American influencers have more reach and followers than me and you, but they are not me or you.

Sometimes I compare myself to them unfavourably because they have ten times as many followers or more podcast listeners than me. What I rarely do is compare how many properties they have, compared to the 750 plus tenants I have a partnership and financial interest in. Or how good their seven-year-old is at golf, compared to my son. They will be doing the same, comparing themselves to Arnie or Leo Messi who has 100 million Instagram followers.

They are great at being them. I admire them and try to learn from them. I used to want to be them, but that is no longer the case. Because I am me, and that's good enough. In fact, it's great. And writing this is hard for me, so it is a forced exercise that you should do, too. Write and share some of the great things about you. I have to tell myself this frequently when I compare myself or talk myself down. I am not my downloads or followers. Whether I have one or one million, it doesn't change who I am.

OK, therapy session for Rob over, but I am sure I am not alone in feeling this – in forgetting all the life experience that makes up who we are, and that it is already enough to add significant value to the world.

Let's face it, others are honouring, owning, packaging and selling their life's work and value, so why can't you? Some are even blagging their way through. We all have a story, and all relate to a compelling story and are inspired by the lives of others. So make sure that you are telling the world *your* story. The story of your whole life that fills you with worth, experience and wisdom that can inspire, serve and add value to other people's lives, too.

As a former struggling artist myself, the Picasso story reminded me that I didn't undercharge for my work because of the market, my recency as a professional artist, my belief about what others could afford and all the other lies I told myself; it was because I undervalued not just my current situation but everything I had gone through in my life. It was this single thing that suppressed my prices and repelled wealthy clients. There's more on how your life's work and self-worth reflect in your prices and earning power in Part 6.

You don't have to go shouting and bragging about it, just own it. If someone gives you a compliment, the best response is to gratefully receive it and allow the giver the joy of giving. Give yourself the same gift: your life's work is your self-worth.

PART 3
What others think of you ...

22

... is up to them

Most of us buy into our individual right to freedom of speech and thoughts. Yet many become hypocrites regarding this freedom when being criticized or challenged. Or when you don't agree with them. It's as if everyone is entitled to *my* opinion. If we want our own freedom of speech and thought, then we have to allow the same to others, no matter how much we disagree, or how strongly it challenges our own views and values.

Of course it hurts when people criticize, troll and hate us. No matter how strong you are, or how thick your skin is, it still hurts. Just this morning I had this one-star review of my book *Money*. I put ten years' research and struggle into that book, and it took me the best part of a year of my life to write, research, check, double-check and edit.

A decade ago, a one-star review or critique on social media would have ruined my day. It often consumed my weekends when I was supposed to be switching off. It could spill over into relationships and into my work. It could even get me to start to question what I was doing and who I was. This is madness.

No one can make you feel anything about yourself that you don't already feel about yourself.

If you get easily offended, side-tracked or consumed by what others say and think about you, that can say more about you than them.

No one can upset or piss you off without your permission.

Once I gained more of a balanced perspective, owned who I was, filled my own self-worth voids rather than constantly needing it from others, I realized these one-star reviews, and all other forms of critique, can be viewed as valuable lessons:

- I'd rather know what people think about my book and why it doesn't work for them, so I have all the information to hand to make improvements for the next book.
- If I had all five-star reviews, my ego would be happy but it might look fake.
- It keeps me in check and balanced, so I don't get cocky when writing the next book.
- My fans don't usually give me feedback to improve, I've learned more from critics.
- The bad reviews get talked about the most and as such are great for my marketing.
- They probably got some therapy leaving the review so I have helped them.
- It gets me to check in with my values to make sure I am being congruent.
- It toughens me up for the next, bigger round of challenge and critique.

Critics have a valuable purpose (there's more on this towards the end of this part of the book). Aside from all these great benefits you get from critics, and those who give you opinions you don't agree with, and how it can make you feel, the opinion of others is actually quite irrelevant to what you are trying to do. Their opinion of you has no bearing on, and doesn't change in any way, who you are. As long as you don't let it.

Churchill said: 'You will never reach your destination if you stop and throw stones at every dog that barks.'

Let others' opinions be theirs; it is their right. You can misread their meaning. You can take it personally when it really isn't. You are likely to be emotional when getting distracted by others' opinions, which can put them out of context. People's opinions say more about them than you; you simply trigger a deeper emotion in them that they already held. Often, they are lashing out because of their own pain, and judging themselves more than you. Understanding this actually connects you closer to your critics. If you can empathize with them, it also helps with how you feel about yourself.

Other than for constructive feedback, don't let others' opinions of you distract you from where you want to go in life. It is quite irrelevant. If you need their approval, then there are other chapters in this book that deal with that issue. Practise letting things go. Accept and be grateful that we all have freedom of speech and opinion. That is how it should be. Transfer all that wasted time and energy trying to control what others think about you into your vision, mission and passion. Someone else's opinion is none of your business anyway, you nosey parker you.

23

Fear of being judged, looking stupid, making mistakes …

Imagine for one idyllic moment that you gave absolutely zero fucks about what anyone thought about you. Imagine all those things you might do that you'd been previously scared about. Imagine all the liberation of wasted time and energy. Imagine all the freeing up of thoughts and doubts and voices in your head. Imagine.

No matter who you are, people will have an opinion on you. Simultaneously, people will love and loathe you. Support and challenge you. Lift you up and drag you down. No matter who you are, or what you say, you will have fans and haters. The things you hate about yourself, others will love. The things you love about yourself, others will hate. If you changed, all that would happen is that different people would love you and different people would loathe you.

I used to think as I got better, fewer people would hate me. Ha! What an idiot I was. The reality is that the better I get, the better known I become and the more I put my true self out to the world, the more critics I attract. The more people see my face, the more people there are to hate my face. Even if only 2 per cent of people who know of me loathe me, which is a low percentage (I'm sure it's more than that), 2 per cent of a million is 20,000 people who hate my face. Two per cent of 10 million is 200,000 haters who hate my face. And this is normal!

How most people avoid all this is by hiding away and playing small. If only 100 people know them, then 2 per cent is only two people. But why should you stay small and not show the world who you really are, just to hide from a few critics? What about the 98 people who admire and respect you? What about the 980,000 or the 9.8 million? What about the 2,500-plus five-star reviewers?

The things that people criticize about you – your apparent flaws, weirdnesses and differences – that is what makes you who you are. That is your uniqueness that the world is hungry for. Nine Inch Nails and Marilyn Manson were perceived as weird by most people, at the time they were discovered. But they were also unique and talented.

Benjamin Franklin would open all the windows and stay nude for one or two hours each morning. He believed this would cleanse his body and protect him against disease. (I might try that one!) Thomas Edison wouldn't hire anyone who added salt to their soup without tasting it first. He wanted to hire people who would 'taste' their assumptions before acting on them. Yoshiro Nakamatsu (inventor of the floppy disk and three thousand other inventions) dives underwater and claims 'being close to death' is when his best ideas come to him. See, we are all weird, but that is also what's great about us.

The first car I owned at 17 years old was an F-reg white Vauxhall Astra with rust around the wheel arches. It was what's known in my part of the world as a 'banger'. It even had a choke, which you young cool kids won't even remember. I thought I'd improve it a little, or 'mod it up', as we used to say. So, I had it lowered, put some new hub caps on it and got a K&N air filter fitted. Often, when I'd pull up in McDonald's car park, I'd get called a 'wankaa'.

I thought, 'Right, I'm going to prove you all wrong. I'm going to work hard. I'm going to make sacrifices and get my head down and become a success and buy a nice car, then let's see what you have to say. Then you'll like me.'

A few years lapsed, but from the age of 26 to 30, that's exactly what I did. I worked damn hard and I bought my first Ferrari, the 430 Spider (for cash),★ and carried all those memories and hand gestures I'd received when driving my banger along with me on my journey. I used it as motivation. The day I got it, I decided to cruise down estate agents' row, at '2 miles an hour so everybody sees you' (I might have even been singing the Will Smith song in my head at the time). As I did, I stalled the car not once, not twice, but three times in front of all the young estate agents. As I did, all the hand gestures came back out, and once again I was called a 'wankaa', this time by people in suits.

People will judge you anyway. So you might as well be yourself. You might as well be successful. You might as well be rich. Or whatever you want to be. And drive whatever car you want.

When I was single (which was most of my life until I met my wife) I used to go out. Not out, but out out. I used to tell everyone, 'I'm not looking for anyone', or 'I'm happy on my own', and both those statements were complete bare-faced lies. I wasn't into dance music. I didn't actually enjoy drinking, though I gave it a good go. I was lonely and I wanted to meet someone.

Due mostly to all my baggage built up over being the token fat kid at school and the kid who looked the worst in the year wearing Speedo's, I had a big need to be liked. I was really sensitive to rejection, so much so that I would never ask for anything, just in case I got rejected.

★ You will love me or hate me or judge me for the car I drive. Did you judge? Be honest. But it doesn't change anything about me, or how badly I drive it.

Fast-forward to my mid-twenties and this baggage was still almost as strong in me, despite nearly two decades passing and the weight long since shed. I'd go out with the lads, stand at the bar, and hope all night that Tess Daly or Cindy Crawford would approach me and declare their undying love to my face. All I did all night was stand at the bar looking out at everyone. On the rare occasions that a girl looked back and smiled, I'd look down, or, worse, do a double-take behind me. What me? No. OK. Didn't think so.

But the lads loved it. Because I would stand at the bar and look after all the drinks while they went out like a pack of wild animals on to the dance floor to 'pull'. They had absolutely no fear, or shame, about going up to any girl and talking to them. I just couldn't understand how they could do that. The lucky bastards were born with this gift. They'd get blown out repeatedly through the night and wouldn't care less. They'd even laugh when it happened. They'd even go back for more punishment. Jeez if that happened to me I'd want a black hole to form and swallow me into the void of nothingness.

Every night these lads would get a dozen knock-backs, but every night they'd end up with a girl on their arm. Or arms. I'd be all bitter and twisted and jealous (inside) and go home on my own.

For years I'd internally wrestle with this loneliness, struggling to understand why some people didn't care about being rejected or looking stupid. In fact, they seemed to enjoy it. They actually loved getting blown out and looking 'like a twat'. They fed on it. I mean, how? How?

I'm still friends with many of these lads today. And one friend in particular, let's call him Phil (to protect him and hundreds of women across the greater Peterborough area), shared his attitude with me. We'd go on long bike rides together, and he'd ask me how I'd developed a successful business and I'd grill him about his ability to take rejection. He said: 'I just have fun. Life is short. I don't take myself too seriously. And if I get rejected, it's on them, not me. They don't know me. It's not personal. I'm OK with looking stupid. If I ask enough people, someone's going to say yes.'

Wow. Simple. Not simple. It also begs the question, why I didn't ask him back when we going out to bars. Well, I was even scared to ask him. Scared to look vulnerable or stupid, like I should know it all already. Scared of rejection over even asking the question. It seems silly looking back at it.

Our fears of being judged, looking stupid and making mistakes in front of others (society) existed way before societies were even around. We evolved from hunter-gatherer tribes, where judgement from your tribe or clan was all you had separating you from abandonment or exile. This meant almost certain death. As we evolved, we developed very advanced social cues and sensitivity, as a means of ensuring safety and avoiding threats.

These still serve us today, but the threats have changed. Today's threats are social media, keeping up with the Joneses, public speaking, exams, presentations, asking someone out on a date (on Tinder) and job interviews. We find it hard to contextualize them in our mind because we have only a few decades of personal experience and can't just tap into thousands of years of evolution. We literally can't keep up with our environment quick enough.

Due to our living in a more civilized, safe, better-governed society, most of the feelings that result from feelings such as self-consciousness, fear of judgement and scrutiny, inadequacy, embarrassment, humiliation and depression are fictions and figments of our imagination. They aren't real. They're out of date by millennia. They're not happening; we are imagining them.

Have you ever had an argument with someone …

…in your head? Ha! Of course you have. And it wasn't real. You imagined a whole load of shit that they never said, or did, or thought. But it ruined your hour. Or day. Or week. Or life. Imagination can ruin reality. It's kind of nuts to allow this to happen to yourself. It's kind of nuts to take on others' comments, projections or even beliefs about us, when they aren't us. When they don't understand us. Or often when they don't even know us. And when we won't likely die for being ridiculed in modern society.

I would say at least half the time when I thought my supposed school friends were talking about me behind my back, 'you fat fuck', 'Moore's got more rolls than a bakery', and all the other stuff they said (that's the PG version), they actually weren't. Each time they whispered, sniggered or just laughed, I always thought it was about me. I wonder how many times it actually was?

Don't let your strong emotional memories of past events related to how you have been judged or ridiculed, that aren't real, carry into each present and new situation. How insignificant it is to allow how others feel about you, which is totally on them and not you, affect how you feel about yourself. They don't know you. They are simply judging you through their own experiences. You will forever be a victim of your past which will impress negatively on your future, if you allow the opinions of others to affect your own feeling of value.

While I couldn't find a credible research study, some sources state that people actually talk about us for less than 30 minutes a month when we are on their minds, yet we perceive this to be three hours a month. So people are talking or thinking about us five times less than we perceive. They are just far too busy being caught up in their own stuff to be thinking about you.

Set yourself free from the fear of being judged, looking stupid and making mistakes. Stop worrying and start living. Be yourself. They will judge you anyway; you might as well be, do and have what you want.

24
The need for approval

We have a deep-rooted and often complex relationship with authority. It's one of the earliest experiences we have, even before thoughts and words. We primitively respond to the authority figures who take care of us, both familial and societal. After all, our survival is dependent on being protected from danger, both as individuals and as a species, and those who have experience and care for or love us are in the best position to do this. Love and protection ensures our feeling of safety, and any rejection is perceived as a threat.

How our influential authority figures act towards us, and the things they say and do to exert their authority, have enormous impacts on our perceptions of them, and our feelings about ourselves. When they look upon us favourably, with kindness and benevolence, we may come to idolize them. When they are cruel, intolerant and deprive us of praise and approval, we may resist, resent or hate them. If they are ambivalent and indifferent towards us, we can feel neglected and overlooked. Even if they're practising tough love, acting in our own best interests, it can be hard to accept.

We can be easily swayed by kind and survival-ensuring gestures, which can lead to unquestioning respect for authority. We may be eager to please and comply, which can make us susceptible to being manipulated, or to authority figures abusing their power.

Conversely, we can resist and rebel against authority figures, viewing and treating them as hostile and manipulative. We may refuse to comply with rules or instructions, or only pretend to be compliant. Sometimes we may be overly sceptical of the motives of authority figures when they are actually trying to help. Other times we may be naive and susceptible to manipulation due to a blind faith in authority, again stemming from childhood.

Our life experiences in response to authority shape our own desires and conditioning in seeking authority for ourselves. If we've disliked and rebelled against it, we are unlikely to want authority over others. If we've been misled or mistreated by authority figures, we'll be unlikely to want to put ourselves in the same position. If we've loved and respected those in authority, we may crave it for ourselves as a route to love and respect from others.

Our relationship with authority ultimately protects us, but like all things that drain or fill our self-worth battery gauge, it comes with a balance of upsides and downsides. We've all had differing relationships to authority, with an abundance or lack of love in certain areas from certain figures. The upsides of positive authority relationships are:

- control, uniformity and safety, providing order in chaos
- clear rules and boundaries, encouraging discipline
- calm and control in pressure situations
- leadership, productivity, creativity, communication and cohesiveness.

The downsides and results of poor authority relationships can be:

- anxiety and dependency, due to overprotective parents
- lack of social skills, responsibility and resilience

- inability to meet the needs of one's own children due to one's own needs not being met as a child
- insecurities passed down through the generations
- inconsistent authority behaviours leading to confusion and inner conflict
- lack of boundaries leading to a lack of worldly awareness and rules.

This chapter could be an entire book, so to make this relevant to your self-worth, consider questioning the relationships you've had with authority figures in your life:

- Did some of your insecurities originate trying to get love and attention from authority figures?
- Are you trying to get your voids filled by others as an adult that weren't filled as a child?
- Do you have a total lack of respect for authority and therefore live a chaotic, ill-disciplined, rebellious or self-sabotaging lifestyle?
- Are you negatively measuring yourself against your life's authority figures or trying to live up to others' expectations?
- Are you making or avoiding important decisions based too much on the need to please and get approval of others or to not let them down?
- Are you making or avoiding important decisions based too much on the fear of negative or critical reactions of others?
- Are you giving and doing too much for others and not enough for yourself, to impress or please others?
- Are you seeking approval, acceptance and love from people long gone, passed away or relating to events that happened years ago?

Perhaps your need for approval links back to a fear of success and how others will judge you? Or perhaps you don't care enough because you had all the love you ever needed? Take the time to think about your relationship with authority, how it is driving your present behaviours and how you can turn it from holding you back to setting you free.

I'll leave you with this from Nicholas Luca Ricciardi who made this comment about a thread on this subject I started in the 'Disruptive Entrepreneur' community group on Facebook:

Below the age of 22 or maybe even later … I would say conformism really affected me and I have witnessed how it can ruin/limit your life. I would feel I had to do things because it's the social norm or because it's what our Italian family did for generations without anyone questioning it. Fuck that. I am an individual and I will do what I feel is best for me. I will also not believe there is a magical man in the sky because I was told to without having seen any evidence. I believe you have to have a high self-worth to be able to be the rebel and go against what everyone else is doing as it will push people away.

25
OPB – other people's baggage

We all have bad days. Or years. Or fleeting moments. Usually, these bad days poke and pick at emotional scabs covering scars of our past, and we bring them into the present, vomiting them all over other events and people. These people are often those closest to us like our children, family, partner, friends, staff and customers. It hardly seems fair that the people we love are the ones who mostly have to deal with our baggage, but it seems to be the way.

On the one hand, this serves to bring up memories and experiences of the past to save us critical thinking time in the present. If we can draw on past evidence to help us ensure safety or deal with threats, then that time saved could aid our survival. On the other hand, we mix in all our extreme emotions and painful memories in the form of volatile feelings, which can put the present events out of context. To release those emotions and protect ourselves, we lash out.

If we are not aware of this process when we are on the receiving end, we can take it personally. In return, we lash back out and compound the vicious cycle. We then bring up all our own baggage and emotional memory of similar situations, usually that went bad or made us defensive or hurt us, and spit back at the person who spat at us. Each time this happens it can further cloud the actual reality or the situation, with layer upon layer of baggage dumped on top, like pasta in a lasagne. OK, not my best analogy, but I hope you get what I mean.

Imagine each and every event presenting itself to you just as it is, not loaded with wayward emotions. Just clarity and reality.

Imagine how much easier relationships – and in general your journey through life – would be. Imagine how much easier it would be to communicate, solve problems and get things done. Imagine …

I'm going to come back to this in a moment, and how you can take full and personal responsibility for stopping 'the baggage cycle'. But first, let's look at the situations where people dump their baggage on to you. People often:

- feel rejected or hurt, and lash out at you
- hold you down or back through jealousy, envy or 'tall poppy syndrome' – the urge to cut people down to size when they're successful
- try to impose their views and values on to you
- try to make their problems your problems
- want you to fail to feel better about themselves
- feel alone and become needy for help
- take everything very personally and get defensive and resistant to feedback
- explode under extreme pressure in your vicinity (you were in the wrong place at the wrong time).

You can't always control someone's baggage, but you can manage your own. You can take the first step and be the change you want to see by being the first one to stop the baggage dumping process. You can show compassion for their situation. You can show empathy and let them dump their emotions without reacting to them. You can understand why they became emotional and offer your knowledge to help fix the situation. You can listen and be a sounding board, so that the emotional baggage dissipates into the ether because you didn't add to it.

In situations where people are vicious or unfairly critical, you can simply ignore it. Move on. Smile. Even thank them.

Don't take it personally, because you now know it is never about you and always about them.

I had to learn this the hard way, in maintaining two of the most important partnerships in my life, with my business partner and my wife, though not at the same time! I'm the kind of person who seems to piss people off when I breathe, so have had to learn to be sensitive to people and how they react to me (or not me).

My wife's way of dealing with her emotions is to go very quiet, thoughtful and introspective. My business partner's way is to do the opposite and to talk and go over things many times. With my wife, I always used to try to dig in, push and find out what the problem was, because I wanted to help fix it (which is *not* what she wants). This only made things worse, and my emotions would leak into her problem and make it worse.

With my business partner, I used to just tell him that he's told me the same thing about ten times before. I used to try to listen but found it hard to show the interest he needed.

In both situations, I have learned that doing nothing but listening and caring intently is the best way to navigate the issues they both have. When the situations turned into arguments, which turned into explosions, it was because I'd added my own insecurities and emotional reactions, not compassion, to the problem.

This is a lesson I've been learning for 12 years and will continue to work on. I'll probably mess it up from time to time.

I have also learned to not let the others' moods dictate my own. Own your mood, no matter how draining the moods of others can be. This can also affect me as I am quite responsive to the moods of others, but as any kind of leader in family, business and life, your job is to do your best to protect those around you, so they can stay inspired and energized.

There is one caveat to all of this. If you give me a one-star review I am going to dump my whole life on to you. And I have some serious baggage!

26

If you want to be accepted (loved) for who you are …

I had an ex-girlfriend that always used to say to me 'I just want to be loved for who I am'. I think that's as far as we'll go with my past,★ but I think this is such a common phrase and desire; it's a deep-rooted human need.

There is only *one* way to be loved for who you are. That way is *guaranteed* to work for you, if you really want to be loved for who you are. But it is not a short cut. In fact, many people find this one of the hardest things of all to do. I can also guarantee how to *not* be loved for who you are; that is to show the world a false version of who you are. This illusion of self-presentation can be:

- living up to someone else's expectations that aren't your own
- fearing conflict and subordinating yourself to others
- fearing rejection and ridicule and withholding the real you
- self-aggrandizing or over-inflating your achievements
- de-positioning yourself or being overly humble
- showing people the version of you that *you* think they want to see.

★ My ex-girlfriend used to play the famous Goo Goo Dolls song 'Iris' for me: 'I just want you to know who I am'. I should have played her the equally famous CeeLo Green song.

The guaranteed way to be loved, appreciated and accepted for who you really are is simple: show the world who you *really* are. And yes, of course, you risk ridicule, rejection and failure. But you run just the same risk when you show the world a false version of you.

You will attract the people into your life who are attracted to you: life and business partners, customers, followers and fans. These people will (mostly) see what you show them, and will be drawn to you, or repelled away from you, according to the mirror of themselves or their desires that they see in you.

If you show the world a false version of who you are, you attract into your life those people who are drawn to those false traits. It's when this happens that you find yourself surrounded by people whose values do not align with your own, or worse, by false, empty people who offer nothing and drain your energy.

If you are true to yourself you will also attract the odd opposite, whose healthy criticism will keep you in natural balance. If you're not true to yourself, you'll attract your fair share of opponents too – but their contribution will pointless, critiquing a version of you which doesn't really exist.

There will be a little pain, whichever way you choose. You can choose to have a little pain at the start, when you are vulnerable and you risk rejection and ridicule. I get it, it's scary to say, 'I love you' to someone who might throw it back in your face. It's scary to ask for money when you are struggling, because of the judgement you may get. It's scary to say 'I don't know' or 'I can't', or 'Sorry', and admit your flaws and shortcomings.

But the pain later will be greater. The pain of having all the wrong people in your life and having to live a lie. Staying in a relationship you know is over, or a job you've sold yourself out on for decades, or living out the life your parents want for you that you don't.

You can *only* attract the right people and outcomes into your life, when you show the world who you really are, flaws and failings and all.

Remember if you don't value or love yourself, why should anyone else? To value yourself, and show that to the world is not to be a know-it-all or narcissist. It is simply to know your worth and value, your traits and skills, and own them. And accept your flaws, too. Embrace them, and even laugh at them sometimes, as long as they don't hurt others. Don't get too hung up on them. You are doing the best you can with what you know. Show the world confidently who you *really* are. The you that you *know* but don't often show.

27
Forgive them all

Resentment, bitterness, anger, jealousy and hate, while serving a function as feedback, are toxic emotions that will eat away at you, if you let them own you.

I got myself and Mark, my business partner, fired from our last (and only) job. My ex-boss employed me for less than one year many years ago. There was no employment contract, and no formal training or mentoring. There was a phone, a desk and some paper leads placed on our desk. I remember one time my boss spending about £1,500 to get eight cold Google Adwords leads. He put four on my desk and four on Mark's desk: 'Right, Mark, you get four leads; Rob, you get four leads; and you better close them ALL or you're fired.' He then went back into his cave and put his drip back on directly into the £20,000 coffee machine.

He rejected most ideas we offered to him. He got emotional at us randomly. After he fired us, we ended up in the courts over wrongful and unfair dismissal, a process that took an entire year. We eventually won. For at least two years he would talk us down to many people in the industry.

For many years, both Mark and I held some anger, bitterness and resentment towards him and how he treated us. After all, we pretty much ran his business for him, did most of his sales for him, and in return he was very emotional and inconsistent. For up to two years after the split, it looked like his company was doing well. That made the resentment also turn into some jealousy, which at the time I was not honest with myself about.

Thankfully, the million-plus pounds I spent on self-education weren't all wasted on me, and I learned about the power he had over my thoughts and emotions. And I learned that it wasn't his fault and that I had in some sense been responsible. He did the best he could with what he knew at the time. There were many (hidden) benefits in the relationship, and all the more negative emotions were caused by me, not him at all.

At first this was hard to accept. Screw that. But as time went on, and it being the great healer, and his business struggled as ours grew increasingly more successful, as I became a boss and hired people and was able to get a more balanced view, seeing things from his perspective, my emotions changed. At first, I could understand but still held some resentment. Later, doing an exercise of searching for all the (hidden) benefits he had brought to my life turned all that emotion into gratitude. OK, *most* of the emotion!

He hired me with no CV. He was probably pretty much the only person in the world who would hire me other than my family. He gave me the first step and bridge into the property business which completely changed my life. He gave me a lot of freedom considering he was my boss. He could be really funny. He paid for nights out. He let me borrow his Porsche. He introduced me to some great people. I developed my relationship with Mark while working for him. He invested in me. He recommended great books and sent me on courses. He opened my mind. He taught me some disruptive management skills. He taught me a lot about property and business, including a lot of what *not* to do.

The reason he fired us was because he found out that we wanted to leave. He didn't deal with this as elegantly as he could have, but having had many people leave and set up in competition, I now know how this feels. From his perspective, he gave me my chance. He opened the doors. He helped me forge my relationship with Mark, then we both left!

Once I was able to see both sides in a balanced fashion, I had very little to be resentful about, and much to be grateful for. As soon as I went through this process, though I needed some time, there wasn't even anything to forgive. Once I had seen all the experiences from his point of view as an employer, all my negative and toxic emotions just washed away. If I ever meet him again, and he didn't put me in a choke hold, I'd thank him. I might even go in for a man-hug.

Forgive others for the wrongs you perceive they did to you. They don't see it the way you do, and there will be an equally balanced upside to the wrongs you perceive. If you practise compassion and empathy, and see what may be causing how they are acting or reacting, your understanding will help you let go of the meaning you put on it, and your emotions and reactions to it.

Usually when people lash out, they are reacting outwardly to how they feel inwardly. The easiest and most common thing to do is to blame and dump those emotions on people close to them, rather than owning them.

I have found that most often when my staff are getting stressed, getting at each other or have deeper, more serious issues, it is usually because they have problems at home or in their relationships. Or they have health issues they are hiding. Or they feel undervalued. In my early days of management, I'd take their mistakes or performance issues very personally, react to them, dump all my baggage on to them, and put fuel on the fire of the situation. Instead of taking time to consider them, being empathetic and understanding things from their perspective, I would focus on what I wasn't getting out of the employee, or how it was inconveniencing me and my business.

If your son is doing wrestling moves on his sister, he may be getting bullied at school. If someone cuts you up in traffic, they maybe be rushing to hospital to see someone they love who is seriously ill. If someone blames you for something, they may be hurting themselves.

Forgiving others is a practice in:

- taking time to see things from their perspective
- having the compassion and empathy to understand why they are reacting as they are
- disassociating – it's not about you; it is about them
- forgiving them for the inconvenience or pain you feel (publicly, or to yourself)
- examining all the balanced upsides to the situation and see how it has served you
- revisiting a powerful, emotional event, and transforming the pain it caused you so that it gives greater meaning to your life.

If you have experienced really hard and bad things that have happened to you, I understand that forgiveness may not be that simple. This is not about condoning unacceptable behaviours against you, but more about living with and moving on from them. If you have been abused, you may want to see a professional. While I can't advise on a professional basis, I can say that forgiving others is far less about them, or even for them, but for you; to release the hold their behaviours have over you. To release the toxic build-up of emotions that are affecting your life and relationships now and into the future.

Steven McDonald was a young police officer in 1986, when he was shot by a teenager in New York's Central Park, an incident that left him paralysed. He wrote: 'I forgave [the shooter] because I believe the only thing worse than receiving a bullet in my spine would have been to nurture revenge in my heart.' Furthermore, while the younger man was serving his prison sentence, McDonald corresponded with him, hoping that one day the two could work together to demonstrate forgiveness and nonviolence. Unfortunately, the young man died in a motorcycle accident three days after his release, though McDonald still travels the country to deliver his message.

Samereh Alinejad told the Associated Press that 'retribution had been her only thought' after her teenage son was murdered. But in a dramatic turn at the gallows, literally moments before the killer was to be executed, Alinejad made a last-minute decision to pardon the man. She is now considered a hero.

After a long shift at the fire department, Matt Swatzell fell asleep while driving and crashed into another vehicle, taking the life of pregnant mother June Fitzgerald and injuring her 19-month-old daughter. According to *Today*, Fitzgerald's husband, a full-time pastor, asked for the man's sentence to be diminished. He also began meeting with Swatzell for coffee and conversation. Many years later, the two men remain close. 'You forgive as you've been forgiven,' Fitzgerald said.

Nelson Mandela forgave the people who put him in prison for 27 years. Simon Weston, whom I interviewed for my 'Disruptive Entrepreneur' podcast, didn't just forgive but become friends with the man who 'blew him up' and left him physically disfigured for life. In 1981, Pope John Paul II was seriously injured after a man attempted to murder him. He was shot four times during the assassination attempt and had to undergo emergency surgery. After his recovery, the pope visited the prison cell of the man who shot him, reached for his hands, and told him that he was his brother and that he was already forgiven.

I get so moved by stories like this. I can't say I would find this level of forgiveness easy, but I like to think that I might show even half of the dignity and compassion displayed by these amazing people.

Everything is, or has a gift in it, if you take the time to look for it. You have to own what people do to you, or it will own you. If there are people in your past against whom you harbour resentment, anger and toxic emotions, revisit the events that caused these feelings and see how they served you, made you stronger and made you the person you are today. Be thankful, see the upsides, and let it go so you can grow.

28

You can lead a horse to water …

… but you can't make it drink. You aren't responsible for everyone. You can't own people's successes or failures. You can't help everyone or save everyone.

Some people care so much about others. They fear letting them down, or feeling responsible or guilty when things don't go right for them. But the harsh truth is: all you can do is all you can do. You are responsible for your own actions and decisions, but your kids, staff, partners, colleagues – they will all do whatever they want, what is right for them.

The higher expectations you have of others, the more you will likely be disappointed.

It pains me to write this, but I believe this to be the truth: no one is loyal to you. Everyone is only loyal to you when it is convenient to them or it aligns with their values. They will drop you the minute their values get challenged or they get better options.

My staff's loyalty is built on their being able to pay their bills and support their families. I am quite sure that many of my great, loyal staff would leave if a competitor doubled their wages. I am sure my wife would leave me if I didn't load the dishwasher every day. Ha, OK, maybe not, but if the needs she has weren't getting met for long enough, she might well leave me for someone who could meet those needs. Our needs can be very selfish. When our backs are against the wall, and things are hard, we will go into survival mode.

If you are looking to fill a void through other people, you will always be empty. If you are looking to feel better and be lifted up by others, or have your mood or confidence lifted by others, you will mostly be disappointed. This is your responsibility.

Here are some areas where this chapter may be relevant to you:

- You can't save everyone.
- You have to let some people in your life go.
- People will continually let you down (unless you manage your expectations).
- You can't be a charity or hobby business; you have to charge fairly.
- Sometimes the best way to help some people is by not helping them at all (or letting them solve their own problems).
- People's behaviours – and what happens to them because of those behaviours – are not your responsibility (only how you teach, raise or nurture them is).

You can teach but you can't make them do. You can help but you can't solve their problems. You can raise your kids but you have to let them go. You can love someone but you can't make them love themselves. Unless you buy them this book. But then you can't make them read it. Unless you bribe them. Now there's a thought. Read this book or I won't love you anymore. Not tried that one yet. But then I'd hate myself for that. Damn it.

29

Introverts, please stand up

I am not a fan of labels we (or others) put on ourselves. Sure, stereotyping helps us make sense of and filter the millions of pieces of information our brains are being smashed with every second, or whatever, but you can be as wrong about stereotypes as you can be right. Stereotypes and labels are simply time savers. Often, when you create short cuts, there are drawbacks, too.

There are, by definition, no real stereotypes. No two people are exactly the same, and as such no one can fully fit into a single stereotype. Even the lines of what were once thought black-and-white stereotypes, like sex and gender, are blurring. I think it is useful to notice labels and stereotypes you give yourself and others. Use it to save time, but don't make it mean anything specific. The wisdom comes in accepting everyone and everything as if they are new, unique and special.

Might it be true that partners of yours have done things you didn't like, which you saw as similar to an ex, or someone you didn't like? Instead of thinking and accepting that this person is unique, doing something new, you draw on a previous experience and then bring all that baggage forward on to this person and into this new situation. Your brain says, 'This is like that' or 'You are like them', when in fact 'This is only like this'.

One stereotype is that of the introvert. I refute this label. I don't actually think anyone is an introvert, at least not fully. I also don't think anyone is an extrovert, fully. People think I am an extrovert, but this isn't true. I am an extrovert on social media, and sometimes when doing my live talks and videos (although I'd even challenge that – after all who defines when you aren't one and then when you become one). Conversely, in public and around people I don't know and am not comfortable with, I am not an extrovert at all. If you got me talking about business I am pretty confident, but if you sat me in a boardroom with Jeff Bezos, Elon Musk or Jack Ma I would quickly become humble and quiet. If you gave me a mankini and put me at the front of a yoga class, you would see me recede into my shell.

I'm not an extrovert; I'm not an introvert. I'm not what you think I am, and I also surprise myself and am not what I think sometimes. The same is true for you, or anyone you label. Take a techie geek who may be described by others as having 'no people skills', then put them in an online gaming room or code-off or a tech conference, and they quickly rise and shine.

Don't label yourself as an introvert (or extrovert), because you aren't. I know a lot of people, including my very close family, who have owned this label and then let it spread across their entire life. When people do that, they talk themselves out of doing the things they want, love and are great at, because of the fear of being judged, ridiculed, making mistakes and looking like an idiot.

Remove that label, disown it, and all of a sudden you just get out there and live your values, skills and talents. You are good at them, so there's nothing to worry about. You will rise and shine, too. You may even surprise yourself.

Getting yourself out there more will get you more reach, followers, custom and exposure. This will then feed back to you as proof that it, and you, work. It will gain its own momentum and create a virtuous circle in your life. Do not deny yourself a great life because of one shitty and incorrect label. There's more on putting yourself out there in Part 4.

The introvert label will encourage you to hide away, stay stuck, doubt yourself, beat yourself up, be jealous and bitter towards those getting themselves out there, and you will be in a feedback loop of doom which will batter down your self-worth.

If anything, call yourself an 'ambivert'! – an introvert in your areas of lowest skill and interest, as we all are, and an extrovert AF with your skills, talent and genius, as we all are. If you really want to cheat (be smart), partner with extroverts in areas where you are less experienced, and leverage their extrovert label. Do podcasts or articles where no one can see your face and you can edit your content as you see fit. Write books and don't put your face all over it. Be the Steve Wozniak of the partnership. Be Michelle Obama. Be Robin, if you aren't Batman.

Don't tell me you are an introvert and therefore you have no hope, confidence or chance – because I don't believe you.

PART 4

Increasing your self-worth

30
Reverse comparison

'Comparison is the thief of joy,' said Theodore Roosevelt.

I'm going to add to that: 'Negative comparison is the thief of joy.' But imagine if you reversed that comparison. Imagine if you compared yourself (where you are now) to:

- where you used to be (when you were further behind)
- the lowest point you've ever been at or the worst you've been
- other people's downsides or worst traits that you don't have
- other people who have it really hard, way harder than you
- where you *could* have been if you'd have made *worse* decisions
- the *real* version of the person you are comparing yourself to (not the version you perceive)
- others for inspiration only – that is, upward comparison to motivate yourself to be better.

I call this 'reverse comparison' because it is comparing favourably rather than unfavourably. It is lifting ourselves up rather than putting ourselves down. It is motivating rather than soul-destroying, and we rarely give ourselves this gift.

Often, people compare themselves unfavourably to a false version of someone. In a world where people Photoshop and filter themselves, and often show only the edited or best version of themselves, we often don't see all sides and it's easy to believe the only side we get to see. We do not have all the facts.

Chester Bennington, Robin Williams and Chris Cornell all took their own life as I was researching and writing this book. All were hugely successful as deemed by society. On the outside, everything looked fine. Robin Williams, with sad irony, was a comedian. Videos of Chester emerged of him laughing and having fun with friends and family just hours before his suicide. All of them gave millions of people great joy, myself included. It makes me so sad just to write this, but so grateful too that I am still here and I don't have the demons that they did.

You have absolutely no idea what people are going through. For males aged 25 to 44, the number-one cause of death, after accident, is suicide, and it's among the ten leading causes of death in women, too, according to the World Health Organization.

How you see and perceive them is only a very small part of the overall picture. *Everybody* struggles. *Everyone* fights their own demons. *Everyone* gets depressed. It is wise to remember this when you put people on a pedestal and unfavourably compare yourself. You are comparing yourself to an illusion of them that you, others and they themselves have created, without knowing all the facts. This is unproductive and disempowering to your self-worth.

Each time you do this, which you will because we all do and it's human nature, here are some actions to 'reverse' the comparison:

- Each time you put yourself down, talk yourself up (pick five 'ups' for each 'down').
- List out all your strengths when you seem hung up on your weaknesses.
- Pick five things to be grateful for everyday and give thanks for them.
- Read up on the stories of people who've had it *really* hard to give you some context.

- Look back and see just how far you've come and how well you've done.
- Catch yourself out and pat yourself on the back each time you do something good.
- Imagine how badly things could have been had you made (even) worse choices.
- Take an area you're very successful in, and transfer that feeling across to a new project or area of your life.

There are so many people who've had it so much worse than us. Even if you had real trauma, there is always someone far worse off.

Can you guess who this amazing woman is:

- Her mum left her when she was eight.
- Her family was so poor growing up that, as a child, she was teased at school for wearing dresses made of potato sacks.
- She was raped at nine years old.
- She ran away because of sexual abuse at home.
- She became pregnant at 14.
- Her son died soon after birth.
- She was molested by a family friend, uncle and cousin.

I'll reveal who this amazing woman is in a later chapter.

Franklin D. Roosevelt – a distant cousin of Theodore Roosevelt with whom we began this chapter – became partially paralysed at 39. After vacationing in Canada, Roosevelt developed poliomyelitis, which eventually left him paralysed from the waist down for the rest of his life. Even though he couldn't walk, he went on to lead the United States as one of the most respected and memorable presidents in history.

In spite of being diagnosed with amyotrophic lateral sclerosis when he was 21, Stephen Hawking was one of the world's leading physicists and defied doctors for decades.

Nick Vujicic was born without arms or legs. Nick grew up in Australia and, in spite of his disability, he eventually taught himself to do things like skateboarding and surfing. Today he is an inspiring and funny motivational speaker and winner of the Australian Young Citizen Award.

Christopher Reeve, famous for his role as Superman, became a quadriplegic in 1995 after being thrown from a horse. He persisted with his career and, after many dark days and thoughts of suicide, developed a new meaning for his life. He committed himself to philanthropic work as well as his determination to regain movement in his body. He died in 2002 while co-directing *Everyone's Hero* – he is certainly a hero of mine.

There are more light-hearted stories I can offer too. Erik Norrie has been attacked by a shark, struck by lightning, and bitten by a rattlesnake (but not all at once!). The odds of these things happening are 1 in 11.5 million, 1 in 3,000, and 1 in 37,500 (annually) respectively.

A man named Walter Summerford was struck by lightning three times in his life. Four years after his death, his gravestone was struck by lightning as well.

One of the co-founders of Apple, Ronald Wayne, sold his 10 per cent stakes for $800 and left because he found it hard to work with Steve Jobs and Steve Wozniak. Had he stayed on, he would be worth $35 billion now.

You have everything to be grateful for and nothing to compare yourself or live up to, other than that which you demand and desire for yourself. You only compare yourself to someone when you don't know who you are.

Stop comparing where you are to where you perceive you should be, or you feel your parents or authority figures want you to be. Everything is as it should be. Everything is in its right place. Including you.

31

Be your own biggest fan (rather than your worst enemy)

The world will deal you enough critics. It will do a good enough job of beating you up. It will throw all kinds of shit from all angles in your vicinity. You need to do the job of lifting yourself up. So instead of compounding all the beatings you already get, be your own biggest fan. Be in your own corner. Have your own back. Be the founding member of your own appreciation society.

If you don't champion yourself, sell yourself and reward yourself, no one else will do it for you. Instead of being a self-critic and your own worst enemy:

- Pat yourself on the back.
- Gee yourself up.
- Catch yourself out doing things well and let yourself know about it.
- Treat yourself.
- Lavish yourself with praise.

You don't have to tell anyone else. This is a private fan club with one very, very special member. Roll out the red carpet for this VIP and MVP because you are the GOAT.★

★ Most Valuable Player and Greatest Of All Time.

32
Forgive *yourself*, too

The darkest prison that can hold us in captivity for the longest is possibly our own mind. Equally as important as forgiving others is the self-kindness in forgiving yourself, too. If you don't forgive yourself for the mistakes you perceived that you made, and the wrongs that you perceive that you did towards others, they will keep your self-worth from emerging, and you will carry that into your present and future.

Regardless of your past mistakes, you are worthy of anything that any other human being is worthy of. There is no judge and jury of who is worth what, or more or less, than anyone else.

I had a recent one-to-one call where the person I was helping was struggling with his self-worth. He said to me, 'I'm not worth being a millionaire.' But who decides who is worth being a millionaire? Who sets the rules? There are millionaires who are murderers. Millionaires who screw people over. Millionaires who cheat and embezzle. Yet they are millionaires. There are also poor people who murder, screw people over, cheat and embezzle. No one is more (or less) worthy of money, other than those who learn how to make it, own it, keep it and grow it.

People imagine they will be punished in all sort of ways for the mistakes they have made, including being condemned to hell for eternity. (Well, if that's to be true, we are all going there!) These are imaginary beliefs and fears that affect our self-worth. What do many people with religious beliefs do in this instance? They confess their sins and ask for forgiveness.

Asking for forgiveness isn't actually a plea for forgiveness from others. It is giving yourself permission to forgive yourself. It is setting yourself free through the perception that you need to be forgiven by others. You don't in fact need anyone else to forgive you; you just need to do this for yourself. Here are some things to put things into perspective:

- Everyone who has ever lived has made mistakes that you have, or similar, or worse.
- You are not your mistakes and failings; you are you – your mistakes you 'just do'.
- You did the very best you knew how to do at the time you did it.
- You are no less worthy than anyone else. We are all equally worthy.
- You deserve what you get based on merit, not on superstition.
- Where you perceived you wronged others, you equally served them.

This last point is worth exploring. The following happened when I was taking my five-year-old son to his golf lesson. It was 'all going wrong', we were both tired and grumpy, and we were near a road when he started playing up. I tried to calm him down but as he was relentlessly trying to wriggle away from me, I accidentally pushed him and he fell over (though not into the road). I didn't mean for him to fall over, but I did push him harder than I should have. I picked him up, took him to the car, put him in the back and sat myself in the front. We shouted at each other angrily for a few minutes. In ten minutes or so we calmed down a bit, at which point I felt like the worst dad in the history of the world.

The guilt set in hard. While I felt the guilt, I went on to Audible and bought every parenting book I could find. In the next few weeks I listened to them all, on repeat and at two-times speed. While I'm not yet in the running for Dad of the Year, I learned a lot from those books and started practising some of the useful parenting skills I learned.

I also find that when I have lost my cool with my son, I am nicer to and more patient with him over the next few days. He seems to be with me too, as if he, too, regrets our flare-up. Once the emotions subside and you're able to view the situation with a cool head, there are great upsides to my 'shit dad' moments. They show my son where the boundaries are. They force me into learning better parenting skills. They force me into treating him better and with more patience.

Now before I get a load of messages from people slating me for making pushing your kids over an acceptable behaviour, this is not what I am saying. It was an accident, but I was angry. I regret not being calmer, and hope to master those emotions. But that situation served us both just as it caused both of us temporary pain. In this instance, I was able to forgive myself for being a twat as there were benefits, too.

Where you perceive you have made wronged others, you have equally served them. You challenge them and they grow. You resist them and they get stronger. You 'hurt' them and this gives them valuable lessons about toughening up. Many of us believe that everything happens for a reason, so accept this about your perceived mistakes too.

You don't have to punish yourself. Know that your mistakes also served people, and try to be grateful for that. You did your best at that time. Forgive yourself for small things and all things. Show compassion for where you were back then, trying your best and struggling away with good intentions. Be mindful not to beat yourself up and take on the role of a victim by punishing yourself. You have forgiven others, so give yourself the same gift.

33
Your uniqueness and genius

We *all* have a function and purpose in life, something to give to humanity. I believe that to be true, and believe it to be an empowering belief. Even if I am wrong, imagine *not* having any kind of function or purpose in life. In fact, don't. If you are going to believe anything, and if all beliefs are subjective and personal, you might as well believe something that serves you.

If we weren't unique with an individual place and purpose, I believe we wouldn't exist. The challenge to life is that no one is told what that purpose is. We have to go and find it out for ourselves, which seems to be the meaning of life itself – to find our meaning.

One of the reasons many people struggle to both discover and own their uniqueness and genius, is because they measure it against others. They measure it against how society defines genius. Society calls a violinist or scientist or mathematician a genius, and so effectively defines all others as inferior. Such 'geniuses' are simply being themselves, as you are. The differences between these society-defined geniuses and you are:

- They are defined externally as a 'genius'.
- They have concentrated most of their time, energy and values into their area of genius.
- They probably don't feel like, or define themselves as, a genius.

There is no single definition of a genius. How can Messi *and* Einstein both be a genius? Someone who calls one of these a genius probably wouldn't call the other one a genius. We might define a genius as someone who is great or the best; we perceive them to be someone important or useful. Because we all find different things important and useful that means that what passes as genius is subjective.

This means that someone could perceive you as a genius. My sister didn't do as well at school as me, but I have never met anyone on the planet who can make friends with new people as quickly as she can. Within ten minutes of going on holiday she would have a dozen new friends, whereas I was scared to talk to anyone. She has a genius, we might say, for friendship.

Value is subjective. How you value yourself is subjective. Genius is subjective. So:

- Be unapologetically yourself – after all, everyone else is already taken.
- Own your uniqueness and genius.
- Fit in by standing out.
- Remember that what makes you different, or even weird, makes you unique.

People will judge you anyway, so you might as well be and own who you are.

Even though we know we are different, we wonder why we aren't the same. Be aware of the paradox, and don't wish that you were like others. You're not supposed to be.

You matter as *you*.

We are all dependent on each other to survive and thrive as a species, and many people need your talents. There are countless people who are inspired, and need to be inspired by *you*. Your kids, clients, partners, staff, suppliers, employers, followers, fans and even your critics all value, need and love you.

You matter as *you*.

If you ever forget that, or are struggling, then message me on any of my social media profiles. I read all my messages and I will try to help and remind you of the unique genius that you are.

34

Don't fake it till you make it ...

Fake it till you make it? Really?

I think this phrase became popular only because it rhymes. I don't think you should 'fake' anything. I know where this is coming from: you have to think it before you can become it. You have to visualize yourself having, winning or completing the thing before you've done the thing. But there is no need, or benefit, to faking who you are. As a person with integrity you will struggle to fake it, because you will feel like a fraud, and it is not who you really are. But if you do not think about what you want to bring about before it comes about, you will go without.

I think the ideal balance of staying true to who you are, but wanting to become a better person, with better skills, and better results, is best achieved by a replacement of the quote 'Fake it till you make it', with 'Be it till you see it'.

Be yourself now *and* aim to become the future version of yourself you'd love to be. Love and accept who you are *and* have a vision for who you want to be.

It's important to have a personal vision of the person you want to become. We all know how to set goals, though many people don't actually don't do it: in the end not that many people get specific about the person they want to become. You can't master what you don't measure. Not just 'do' goals and 'have' goals, but 'be goals'. The clearer you are on who you are, how you want to be known, who you want to become and how you want to be remembered, the easier it is to live (up to) your values. Clarity becomes reality. You self-actualize.

Dare to dream. Allow yourself to think big and get excited about your future. Never let anyone steal those thoughts from you or make you believe that you can't be them, or shouldn't think them. If you lose your dreams you lose your hope, and if you lose your hope you lose your worth. Dreams become realities and thoughts become things.

My book *Life Leverage* goes into detail about setting a clear vision, values and goals. This book is about helping you know that you are worth more. You are worthy of everything, but because you don't have all that you want yet, 'be it till you see it', don't 'fake it till you make it'.

35
Take (good) care of yourself

As more cavernous wrinkles have appeared on my forehead, and my staff has grown, and as I've attracted more critics and now have little kids biting my ankles, the realization that I am getting older and that life is short is staring me in the face.

I am often asked, 'What advice would you give your younger self?' Well, in addition to 'Stop drinking' and 'Start your own business', it would be 'Take good care of yourself'. What you take for granted now you may wish you still had later.

In this context, I'm not talking about moisturizing and going to the gym. I'm talking about how you talk to yourself, care for yourself and love yourself.

Having self-worth is having good emotional and mental health. If you don't value yourself, you won't care for yourself, and if you don't care for yourself, you won't value yourself. It becomes a self-fulfilling prophecy, as is the reverse: if you value yourself, you'll care for yourself, and if you care for yourself, you'll value yourself.

Treat yourself with the respect you deserve. Honour your values and personal code of conduct. Try the things you want to try in your life. Reward yourself when you do something well. Celebrate when you have wins, both big and small. Spoil yourself rotten from time to time. Talk yourself up. Educate yourself. Train well. Eat well. Rest well. Sleep well. Work well. Have fun. Make love. Play. Laugh. Live.

And if you don't do this all the time, which you won't, don't beat yourself up. Forgive yourself easily. Laugh it off. Go at it again. Try your best. That is all you can do, and that is good enough.

36

The people you spend (the most) time with …

… will largely define who you become. There's a well-known theory that you become most like the five people you spend the most time with. Do the people you spend the most time with, including family, friends, colleagues, partners, bosses and mentors:

- lift you up or drag you down?
- inspire you or drain you?
- support you or hold you back?
- love you for who you are or try to change you to who they want you to be?
- stay honest with you even if you don't want to hear it?
- speak well of you when you're not there?
- teach you and share their experiences openly?
- feel happy for you in success and make sure they are there for you in defeat?
- make you want to be a better person?

Are the people who are advising you on your career successful in their own? Are the people giving you money advice millionaires? Are those throwing around relationship advice in the perfect, happy marriage? Do all those parenting gurus have model children?

Often, free advice is worth every penny. Be strategic, careful and clinical about the advice you choose to accept and base your important decisions on. You may be allowing yourself to be influenced by someone who is throwing bad advice at you, without the requisite experience.

Sometimes they really do care, and they are trying to help. They love you and don't want you to fail, so they tell you not to start up that business or not to take that risk. They say: Stay safe. Appreciate what you have. You have a good life; don't risk your mortgage or your safe job or your happy marriage. They care, but they are simply the wrong person to give that advice.

Often, however, your success and you taking chances and winning big makes them feel small. They realize they have sold out their dreams, and it makes them feel safe and comfortable if you stay right where you are, thank you very much. They get secondary gain from you playing small. They like you just the way you are because it doesn't make them feel bad for who they are. They're like that bucket of crabs that needs no lid because when one crab tries to reach for freedom, the others claw him back in.

To those who really do care, thank them. Show them gratitude, but pick and choose wisely what you listen to and what you reject. You don't have to say anything, just smile. I'm not into all this 'fuck the haters' nonsense every time someone disagrees with you. There are valuable lessons to be had from critics and people you care about challenging you. You don't have to fire all your friends and family just yet.

Because the world is a mirror of who you are, the friends and network you keep are who you've attracted into your life. You are fully responsible for the people around you. A rising tide lifts all ships, and that's how it should be with your friends and network. Genuine friends and the right people who equally add and receive value will stick around. Don't have false loyalty to those who don't really care, just because you have known them a long time. Let them sail in a different direction blown by their own wind, while you set your sail for the golden horizon. Choose your network strategically and wisely.

Love your family (parents, siblings and so on). You can't choose them, but you can control your exposure to them. Choose to discuss things trivial or unrelated to your vision and mission. Change the conversation and protect your mindset, because it significantly determines your behaviours and the results you get. If you hang around with monkeys, you may become one.

The wrong people in your network may keep you safe, but hold you back. They may steal, or aid you in selling out, your dreams. They may not be consciously aware of this. You may not be consciously aware of this. But beware.

It is much harder to change your entire mindset than it is to change your friends and network circles. It is a genuine short cut to success to hang around with inspiring and experienced people. They can help you navigate and avoid the minefield of mistakes and disasters. They can introduce you to experienced and talented people who can open doors for you. You can stand on the shoulders of giants. You can leverage their decades of experience. You can vicariously learn all they did in a shorter timeframe without all the expensive mistakes and trial and error.

Like attracts like. Wealth attracts wealth. Great people attract great people. They say your network is your net worth. While I agree, I don't think it's the full formula. I believe it to be:

$$\text{network} \times \text{self-worth} = \text{net worth}$$

This will be explored further in Part 6.

In my 'Disruptive Entrepreneur' community on Facebook, someone posted: 'Years ago, somebody said to me in a moment of frustration, "How can you fly like an eagle when you're surrounded by frozen chickens!"' I think that just about sums it up.

37
Change one thing; change everything

If you are in a hole, if you feel down and of low worth, if you are frustrated, confused, overwhelmed, wallowing in self-pity and loathing …

Get. Something. Done.

Get one. Thing. Done.

Get. Anything. Done.

Something beats nothing, even if it is the wrong something.

A body in motion tends to stay in motion, and a body at rest tends to stay at rest. This is Newton's First Law of Motion. The object at rest (doing nothing) and the object in motion (doing something) will keep on doing the same thing (still or moving) unless acted upon by each other or another force.

This law of motion is really simple. Of course, when you are feeling completely unmotivated or undervalued, it's not so simple. Often, we put this big wall or mountain in the way; we perceive the task is big and hard and scary. We're in a deep low. The void is vast. It is at those moments that it's wise to remember that all you need to do is something. *One* thing.

How do you eat an elephant? One bite at a time. How do you run a marathon? One step at a time? How do you write a book? One word at a time.

On the subject of books, writing a book is hard. You'd think, this being my fourteenth book I've been involved in writing, that it would get easier. Or I would get better. Well, no. It's just the same. Raising kids and writing books are up there in my top five hardest things to do. It doesn't get any easier. But my way to get the book done never changes: write one word at a time.

In my book *Start Now. Get Perfect Later*, I discussed the demons I go through every time I write a book. The constant screaming in my head telling me to do *anything* else but write the book. There's the *epic* procrastination and task jumping that I wrestle with every time. It's part of the book writing process (for me), but the result is always the same. Start writing. Every day, start writing. Write. Editing comes later. Feedback comes later. Publishing comes later. But all of these become never unless you open a blank document and start writing.

Action breeds action, which creates momentum, which breeds more action. Start now. Get perfect later.

I once interviewed one of the best hostage negotiators and preventers of suicide in the UK on my 'Disruptive Entrepreneur' podcast. She has dealt with a vast number of suicide cases and saved numerous lives. She told me that when people have three bad major life events happen at once that's when they can get very depressed or even consider suicide. She said that most people can handle one or even two misfortunes, but any more and they are likely to take a nosedive. I asked her advice on how someone goes about dealing with that and she said: 'Start with one thing. Get one tackled first. Not all three, that's too much.' Get one thing sorted, or started. Once one is solved or at least on the way to being solved, the stress reduces, the overwhelm diminishes, the mist clears and the momentum reverses.

Don't worry about tomorrow, or the second thing on the to-do list. Just start or change one thing. Pick one area of your life that is important to you, where your self-worth is low, and start there. Send out your CV. Go and hug your kids and read them a story. Invest in that course you really want to do. Make the next meal you order a healthy one. Get in the car and drive to the gym. One little thing can have a domino effect of changing every (big) thing.

38

Get something meaningful or challenging done

This can at first glance seem to contradict the last chapter. That's OK, because everything exists in paradox. If you are to pick one thing to get started, make it something meaningful. Just like getting something done gives you momentum, getting something meaningful done also gives you momentum. It also gives you reward.

Firstly, doing something meaningful physically stops you doing something trivial and superficial. Getting stuck in trivialities will likely reduce your self-worth battery gauge temporarily, which facilitates getting nothing done of any substance. Don't let the small things get in the way of the big things.

In our business park which houses our office and training facilities, there are a couple of business owners who have appointed themselves the parking police. As soon as someone parks out of place, even by an inch, out they rush waving their finger in the air and creating a massive scene. They go around rallying the troops and sit in committee meetings taking up half their time dealing with parking complaints. Their title: jobsworth.

No laws have been broken. There has been no catastrophe. No one has died. In fact, half the time their accusations are handed out to the wrong people. But still out they come, like they have fitted motion sensors to the yellow lines and are sitting in their pants in a dark room full of screens 24 hours a day, waiting to catch you out if you break wind in your car.

I am convinced it's because they are bored. As well as looking to boost their sense of self-importance perhaps. But they clearly have nothing better to do, because if they did, they would be doing it, and wouldn't give a toss about where you park.

The lesson here is: the menial will get in the way of the meaningful if you let it, so don't. Look out for where you're being pedantic and have become the self-appointed police of the trivial, and fire or retire yourself fast.

The second benefit of getting something meaningful done is that you get great rewards. This reward, in the form of 'happy' chemicals produced by the brain, gives you the momentum to do more. The feeling is very addictive. It's meant to be.

The scientist David J. Lieberman, who wrote *The Science of Happiness*, describes happiness as 'the continual progression toward meaningful objectives'. The four primary chemicals of happiness in the brain are dopamine, oxytocin, serotonin and endorphins. They are released when you make 'forward progress towards meaningful objectives'. This is a very specific sentence with carefully chosen words.

They key thing here is that the reward is relative to the meaningful nature of the task. This explains why you feel elated when you have done something really hard. Maybe you know what it feels like to complete a marathon, or drag yourself out of debt – anything really well fought and hard earned. Like finishing a bloody book.

The problem with the 'just be happy' claptrap is that there is little reward for trivial and unimportant tasks. No one feels elated when they seal an envelope or waste time on social media. Getting something easy done, or nothing at all, provides little reward. Greater feelings of elation come from struggling through something hard and meaningful and defeating or completing it. You can feel you are at the point of 'make or break', and when you break through that pivotal moment, when it could have gone wrong, you grow, you become more independent and your self-worth increases in line.

The 'struggle' is an inextricable part of that process. In the instant world of light-speed internet, one-click ordering and livestream social media, we have become so impatient, that we often try to avoid the struggle for the quick fix, short cut or cheat. There's a big difference between a genuine short cut, like getting a mentor or following a proven process already stress-tested, and a get-rich-quick or idle-lazy-bastard one, like expecting results to come without effort or income without investment.

I remember the sweet taste of ultimate freedom when I passed my driving test. I will never forget that feeling. It felt so sweet because I had wanted freedom since my early teens. I spent years dreaming of having my driving licence. I spent months taking lessons. The lessons were hard. My driving instructor was tough on me. I was so nervous about the test. All the struggle built up and then that moment when I got my licence ... well, if only you could bottle and sell the feeling I got; I'd buy it from myself.

The struggle serves us to:

- create a great context for, and contrast to, success
- reward us for meaningful work, so that we continue to do meaningful work
- teach us value and worth
- build up character traits like resilience
- weed out those who don't have the stomach for the fight or aren't up to the job
- focus our minds on both the need to break through and succeed

- skill us up and give us greater tools and experience
- value experiences and people and give back (support, teach, donate, inspire)
- show us who we really are and what we are really capable of
- make things easier and better next time and prepare you for the next bigger challenge.

I witness so many people jumping from easy short cut to easy short cut in the hope of faster results, only for it to be a long cut because of all the time wasted jumping around from thing to thing and starting and stopping and chopping and changing. Each time you start again, again and again, you have to go through all the same chaos again. It. Does. Not. Get. Easier. There is some smart, famous advice for people stuck in this magnetic black hole: 'Stop wishing it were easier; wish you were better.'

It gets easier when you push through the struggle and chaos. If you go through this cycle of looking for the easy way, break the pattern. Are the distractions a way of staying safe and comfortable and avoiding the pain of difficult activities? Call yourself out for active procrastination (but don't beat yourself up about it).

- Hold your breath and pick up the phone and make that sales call.
- Go and see the person you need to apologize to and look them in the eye.
- Deal with the nasty customer complaint first before all other admin.
- Block out all easy and convenient distractions and do that deep, focused work you've been putting off since 1985 …

And know that when you get started, you will gain momentum, and as you make progress you will feel great.

Every person on the planet that you look up to has this same internal and external struggle. Every overnight success took ten years or more. Every graceful ballerina has plasters and sores all over her feet.

39
Master something (one thing)

Anything. Your thing. Something. One thing.

At school, I was half decent at most things and really good at nothing at all. It got me by, but the kids I admired at school weren't half decent at everything; they were great at one thing. You could see how even the kids who were perceived as geeks, or lacking in confidence, came to life and puffed their chest out when they did their thing better than anyone else.

One of my best mates, Dave, is a pretty quiet guy. He was the best at Maths in our year. Everyone knew it. It gave him visible confidence. He turned into a grander, more confident version of himself, sometimes even becoming cocky and argumentative, when Maths was the subject. It gave him a swagger, a glow; his walk even changed slightly.

I am convinced that the world disproportionately rewards not those who are good at a few things, but great at one thing. I believe that inner confidence and worth come from knowing that you have strength, skill and value. This is rewarded by society because the best in their fields serve humanity, steering it towards its greatest potential and capacity.

It doesn't really matter which one thing you master. It can be a passion or profession. Of course, if it can bring you great joy, make you millions and be of great value and service to others, then that's great. But behind this what matters is the feeling of inner worth you get from that mastery. Your ability to be confident in that one area you can then transfer that into other areas.

Success leaves clues, and anything you have to endure to master one thing will leave its trace on everything you do.

In Chapter 6 (How *you* value something), we discussed the weird and wonderful, quirky niches that people had become very successful in and monetized handsomely – even if, superficially, they appeared to be out of the 'mainstream'. Here are some more, evidence that you can master one (weird) thing:

After hearing his friends in a bar complain about the responsibilities of pet ownership, Gary Dahl conceived the idea of the Pet Rock – a small stone that was marketed as a low-maintenance companion. They came with minimal decoration and came with an owner's manual. It was a great big hoax and all of America wanted to get in on the joke. He sold 1.5 million of the Pet Rocks in one year at a price of $4 per rock, with very few overheads.

Two brothers, unemployed and without a college education, started a business in the middle of a recession by selling meat from farms to consumers in a church parking lot. The idea quickly grew into a $70 billion business. Talk about bringing home the bacon.

Ailin Graef, better known through her online alias of Anshe Chung, earned $1 million by selling virtual real estate in the online game 'Second Life'. It was based on her character's net worth of 'linden dollars' in the game.

Kuro Takhasomi (KuroKy) turned his disability into his passion. He goes by the gaming handle KuroKy and is the current highest earner in the eSports arena, with a total earnings of $3,480,788.35 to date. Kuro suffers from a disability that makes movement difficult, and he says that it was this disability that led him into gaming and on to this great 'career'.

Philadelphia brothers Bernard and Murray Spain bought the legal rights to the yellow smiley face, along with the now-infamous tagline 'Have a nice day.' The brothers began slapping the image on everything possible. The yellow smiley swept the nation and, soon, the world. The fad peaked in 1971 and diminished after a year and a half, but that was enough time to make $50 million in sales. Later, in the 1980s, they opened the first Dollar Express where they continued to sell the smiley. In 2000 they sold their chain to Dollar Tree for $500 million.

Fill a sack with beans, give it furry ears, and name it something cute. The result? A toy empire bigger than Hasbro and Mattel combined. Beanie Babies, founded by Ty Warner, sold 30,000 units at the first toy show in Atlanta. At the peak of the Beanie Baby craze, Ty reportedly raked in $700 million in one year and had made an estimated total profit of 3–6 billion dollars.

I love these stories. There are so many of them. We assume that we need to master the popular or the conventional or the proven, but you can literally master virtually anything.

My dad gave me complete freedom, support and finances to do whatever I wanted. I will be forever grateful to him for that, but the downside was that it was always pretty easy for me to give up on something or start something new. I'd look at something else someone else was doing that I'd want to be good at. I'd get jealous, then excited, then committed. I'd go at it hard like a handbag dog humping a leg, get half decent at it, then the struggle would set in. The mastery part, where you get diminishing returns on effort, would take longer and get harder. Right at that point, like a magpie, I'd see something else and off I went humping a different leg. The pain of the struggle was released, and the naive excitement (and belief that this time it would be easier) would kick in.

I have played most sports, got to brown belt or better in three different martial arts, and tried a few careers. If I'd put just half of that effort and energy into one area, even a quirky area,

I'd be better known, perhaps perceived as being more successful or at master level. Brown belts don't become UFC champions. Hobbyist sportspeople don't play for their country.

While it could be said that reaching for those heights is unrealistic, I'm convinced that, if I'd focused and honed all my energy into one thing, that success would have come. Thankfully, after a couple of false starts, I got started running my own business. Being an entrepreneur is one area where you can be a 'generalist specialist'. As is being author, influencer, interviewer, social media commentator, or a coach or consultant.

So, after 35 years of (soul) searching, I feel that being a generalist specialist is something I can own. Being prolific rather than perfect. Being an overseer rather than an undertaker.

This has been very liberating. I share this story because you can pick either road. You can work on a skill or area that inspires you and become great at it – even if its Beanie Babies or Smiley Faces or gaming. Or, if you have struggled to 'find your why' and find your 'one thing', then you can be a generalist specialist. You can be a founder, leader, 'leverager' and steerer. You can have a basic knowledge of many (related) things, and then align with, inspire and leverage those who are masters and experts.

I used to get these high highs when starting the new thing. These would be very superficial and would turn quite quickly into a diminished sense of my own self-worth as I moved on to the next thing, more in hope than expectation or belief. This pattern can take a bar off your self-worth battery life each time. While it is true that you can work on your inner self-worth now, with little external proof or validation, you will get a great boost when you get good at something. That proof will then feed back and transmute into other areas of your life.

When I got out of debt, my personal and social confidence also went up. That debt was built up over seven years, so it was like being liberated after seven years of pain. When I learned good management and marketing skills, the rising of those tides lifted up many other areas of my business and beliefs about it. I felt more ready and confident for any challenge thrown my way – staff or legal issues, the economy, regulatory changes or even a big recession.

Then, as that self-worth feedback loop compounds, you then feel worthy enough to teach others. I get much of my pleasure in business nowadays not from the things I personally achieve, but the things my team individually and collectively achieve. This adds to that feedback loop of self-worth, and it keeps on growing. The feeling of being in a position to help, lead and inspire others is one of the best feelings life will grace you with. In addition to a higher and deeper sense of unshakable self-worth, you also feel gratitude, which is the cure-all emotion for any pain and suffering.

Do your very best to master one thing – be it a specialism or a generalism.

40

Failure *is* success

The harder I tried, the luckier I got. I succeeded the most because I failed the most. Michael Jordan and Gary Player, and many successful people before them and after, have attributed their attitude to and experience with failure *as* their success.

Most people, with their fears and ego, perceive failure as failure. But, as we all know, when we take the emotion out of it, the only way to succeed BIG is to fail over and over and over again.

My friend Terry would end up with a girl (or two) on his arm at the end of the night because he would take knockback after knockback with a smile on his face. For every 100 properties I have viewed, I have failed to buy at least 85 of them.

I think right up there in my all-time favourite 'failure' stories is this one. Can you guess who this is (if you haven't heard me talk about it already)?

- He failed in business at age 21.
- His mum and sister died.
- He was defeated in a legislative race at age 22.
- He failed again in business at age 24.
- He had a total nervous breakdown and was bedridden for six months.
- His sweetheart died at age 26.
- He went bankrupt
- His first son died at age four.
- He had a nervous breakdown at age 27.

- He lost a congressional race at age 34.
- He lost a congressional race at age 36.
- His second son died at age 12.
- He lost a senatorial race at age 45.
- He failed in an effort to become vice-president at age 47.
- He lost a senatorial race at age 47.

... And was elected president of the United States at age 52.

Can you guess who it is? I'm not telling!

Sylvester Stallone bounced between foster homes and low-paid jobs while his parents endured a troubled marriage. Things got so bad that he even ended up homeless. He slept at the New York bus station for three days, unable to pay rent or afford food. He even tried to sell his dog at the liquor store to any stranger. He didn't have the money to feed the dog anymore and sold his dog for just $25. He says he walked away crying.

Two weeks later, he saw a boxing match between Mohammed Ali and Chuck Wepner, and that match gave him the inspiration to write the script for the famous movie *Rocky*. He wrote the script for 20 hours and tried to sell it. He got an offer for $125,000 for the script. But he had just one request: he wanted the lead role in the movie. The studio said no; they wanted a real star. They said that he 'looked funny and talked funny'.

A few weeks later, the studio offered him $250,000 for the script. He refused. They even offered $350,000. He still refused. After a while, the studio agreed, gave him $35,000 for the script and let him star in it. The rest is history. The movie won Best Picture, Best Director and Best Film Editing at the prestigious Oscar Awards. He was nominated for Best Actor, and the movie was inducted into the American National Film Registry as one of the greatest movies ever.

And do you know the first thing he bought with the $35,000? He stood at the liquor store where he'd sold his dog, for three days, waiting for the man he'd sold his dog to. He saw the man coming and explained why he'd sold the dog. He begged for the dog back. The man refused. Stallone offered him $100. The man refused. He offered him $500. And the guy refused. He refused even $1,000. In the end Stallone had to pay $15,000 for the same dog he sold at $25. He also gave the man a part in *Rocky*.

At 17 years old Justin Rose shot to fame by taking fourth place in The Open (one of the four major golf championships). He turned pro the next day with the world at his feet. He then missed the cut in his first 21 consecutive events. He earned his first European Tour card in 1999 when he finished fourth at the qualifying school. The following season he failed to retain his card and had to revisit the qualifying school.

In 2003 Rose reached number 33 in the Official World Golf Ranking. He did not have a great year and slipped out of the top 50 in the world rankings. His ranking continued to fall until early 2005, and in March of that year he announced that he was quitting the European Tour and concentrating on playing on the PGA Tour. This had no apparent effect on his poor form, and by the middle of the year he had fallen out of the world's top 100.

In 2018 he gained the world number-one ranking, won the $10 million Fed Ex Cup and won the Ryder Cup.

One of the world's most iconic and beautiful women was told early on by a modelling agency that she should consider being a secretary instead. She struggled to get successful roles and was fired by 20th Century Fox because her producer thought she was unattractive and couldn't act. She spent her childhood in foster homes and orphanages. At one point, she worked in a factory as part of the war effort in 1944, then met a photographer and began a pin-up modelling career. Her modelling led to two short-lived film contracts with 20th Century Fox and Columbia Pictures and a singing career. By the time of her death, her films grossed $200 million.

Can you guess who she is? No, not telling.

'Success', Winston Churchill quipped, 'is going from failure to failure with no loss of enthusiasm.' How right he was.

We need to flip failure and the perception of it on its head. Failure is success. Success is failure. In every single success story there are failure stories like the ones outlined above embedded in them. I love them. They motivate the hell out of me. They make me want to fail more and more (unintentionally, of course).

Taking this idea one step further, not only is failure success, but accidental failure often leads to accidental success.

In 1879 Louis Pasteur and his collaborators discovered that injecting old, discarded cultures of cholera into chickens made them more resistant to cholera. This occurred while they were testing for something completely different. Christopher Columbus was looking for a new way to India in 1492 and wound up landing in the Americas. The Kellogg brothers accidentally discovered corn flakes in 1898 when they left cooked wheat unattended for a day and then obtaining a flaky material instead of a sheet when they rolled out the mass.

Percy Spencer was testing a magnetron for radar sets and noticed that a peanut candy bar in his pocket had melted when exposed to radar waves. From this accident, the microwave oven was invented. A Canon engineer rested his hot iron on his pen by accident. Ink was ejected from the pen's tip. This led to the creation of the inkjet printer.

Embrace failure. Try your best, but accept the failure and stay open-minded so you can learn from it. Who knows what you might discover. I now have more than 300 one- or two-star reviews for my books. (I clearly need therapy around my book reviews. I even took time out of writing this book to count them all. I must be grateful for them!) That's a lot of bad reviews, but only around 3 per cent of all the total reviews.

Know that each failure is part of the building blocks of your success. Sure, try the best you can, but also dust yourself off and try again. Don't take your failures too seriously. Stay humble, curious and consistent. Failure is not failure; failure is success.

41

Your non-negotiable code of conduct

In Part 1 of this book we discussed one of the definitions of self-esteem being 'confidence in one's own worth or abilities; self-respect'. This raises two additional concepts that make up part of who you are: self-confidence and self-respect. When you are 'full' in these areas, or at least not completely empty, it becomes much easier to live up to your values and your personal code of conduct. You no longer feel that you let yourself down or get cornered into things you don't want to do. It becomes easier to accept the right things into your life and eject the wrong ones out of it. Your vision, priorities and time management become ever more crystal clear and unwavering.

Your self-esteem, confidence and worth are dovetailing self-concepts that drive the way you feel about, and how you see yourself in, the world we live in. How you compare to everyone else. How you measure up to and measure yourself against what you think a decent human being should be. How much you feel that you are living with integrity, value and honour. The extent to which you can trust your abilities, qualities, and judgement. How much courage you have to know yourself, believe in yourself, and act with conviction.

Life will constantly throw things at you that will increase and challenge your self-worth, but the thing you can do to best protect and increase it is to have a personal code of conduct – your personal standards by which you live and the traits and qualities that make you feel good about yourself. Once defined, these act as the defensive wall around your esteem, confidence and self-worth. They help you to self-actualize and become the person you want to be, someone whom you'd admire.

It is not for me to say what these standards and codes of conduct are, because they are very personal. I suggest you link these to what's most important to you; – your personal, family and brand values. You could consider:

- acting in a consistent manner
- sticking to your word
- treating people how you'd like to be treated yourself
- saying no to things that violate your boundaries
- making your priorities your priority, above all else.

Conversely, do your best to avoid things that violate this personal moral code and ultimately your self-worth (without beating yourself up when you let things slip from time to time). These might include, for example:

- general things that feel good in the moment but have a 'come down' or cause regret later
- talking badly of people unnecessarily
- bad time and appointment management
- putting others unnecessarily ahead of yourself
- letting the menial get in the way of the meaningful
- letting your emotions get the better of you.

Set some rules for yourself based on your increased self-awareness. Make sure that these rules and the standards that you commit to make you feel good about yourself. Balance the value you give to the world with the energy you need to take care of yourself.

In the early days, I used to commit to responding to every message and email I got. I was grateful that people wanted to ask me questions, it adhered to our brand values of being 'personal' and it made me feel good and valuable. As my reach grew, this became harder and harder to maintain, to the point where it was encroaching on my own time, and I was starting to get frustrated. So, over time, I reset my rules, going through the following stages:

1 Reply to all messages.
2 Reply to all nice messages.
3 Reply to all the clear, concise messages.
4 Reply to as many messages I can in the time I put aside to help.
5 Train someone to reply on my behalf and use rules 1–3.
6 Any messages where the answer was in my books or podcasts, point them in that direction with the promise of an individualized answer if they still add questions afterwards.
7 If anyone is ever in real trouble, *always* respond personally.
8 When I have time, or am bored, allow myself to reply and help randomly.
9 Collate the common questions/problems and create a talk, video or podcast to help more people.
10 Train a second person as outlined in stage 5.

I'd like to remind you of the 'law of lesser pissers': if you're given the choice between pissing someone else off or pissing yourself off, choose them every time. People come and go, but you're with you for the whole trip.

Have a clear non-negotiable code of conduct. Own it. Ignore how other people judge it. Balance being selfish and selfless. Hold yourself to a high standard and do your best not to let yourself down, or it will drag your self-worth down with it. On the rare (or common) occasions that you do, forgive yourself easily, and check in with your personal code of conduct and tweak if necessary.

42
Say no. Or 'Not now'. Or 'Never'

Having self-worth and respect is about having boundaries that you do not allow yourself to cross. And, equally important, it is about having boundaries that you do not allow other people to cross.

On the face of it, saying yes is accommodating, polite, pro-active and positive. Under the surface, if you say yes to things that overstep your boundaries, you will:

- create too many commitments you can't stick to
- feel overwhelmed and frustrated at the world (with friends, customers, fans)
- act out of obligation not consideration, choice and compassion
- let people down when you can't deliver (even if well meaning)
- reduce or ruin the quality of your output
- build up resentment, guilt and stress
- sort out other people's emergencies to the detriment of your own priorities.

It is not anyone else's fault if things get out of hand. It is fully your responsibility. You choose what you accept into and reject from your life. You choose what you say yes and no to, no matter how much someone might try to influence you. The words come out of your mouth. You have taught the world how to make demands of you, based on how you have previously behaved and responded, and what you have accepted and rejected.

People learn fast. If they sense you will bail them out, they will rely and lean on you to do it again. They will come to you, rather than solve the issue themselves. In extreme cases, they will become dependent on you, and start to drain you of a few pints of your blood. I know I rely on and ask people who I know will say yes. Staff and outsourcers I have who don't (or can't) say no, I naturally give them more and more. I will only stop if they push back, and I might even push back if they push back.

You want to be helpful in the moment. Or you have fears around saying no. Or you have some secondary gain for saying yes. So you say yes. And yes. And yes. Yes to everything. You may say yes, because:

- you want to be known as someone who is helpful, kind and supportive
- you fear rejection, judgement or ridicule
- you fear you may miss opportunities
- you don't want to let people down
- you are actively procrastinating about your own important (but hard) tasks
- you get a secondary gain for helping others.

The secondary gain you may get could be that you are avoiding the hard things by saying yes to the easier things, as a way of distracting yourself. It might be the martyrdom of being the person who comes to everyone's help and saves the day. 'Look at me, everyone. I always come to the rescue. Over here, look at me.'

It might be your way of perceiving value and self-worth. It might even be a way of getting people's love. That's all fine when it's in balance, where you serve both yourself and others equally. When you get your important work done first. Where you have already collected your fees, and served those who pay you and require your services. I like to ring-fence about two hours a day for helping people, answering questions, calls and giving back. That way I'm in control, and it's not interrupting the things I need to get done myself, and I can be fully present. Then when I say no there is far less guilt, because I know I have given what I can, maybe more.

Remember the law of lesser pissers from the last chapter (there's a lot about this in my book *Money*). If you have the binary choice between pissing yourself off or pissing others off, pick them every time. Say no, politely but firmly. Yes, you risk upsetting them, but that's on them and not you. If you piss off yourself, you will lash out and piss everyone else off anyway!

I get hundreds of messages a week, and I am very grateful for that. However, while it's a tiny percentage, about one a week slips through the net that gives the impression that my sole purpose for being born on this earth is to serve the writer's every need and desire. And at the speed of light and for free. It's as if I should be on high alert to react to their every whim. As if I should be peeling them grapes and fanning their face. I'm a successful entrepreneur, so I should be 'giving back'.

Sometimes I feel like I want to tell them how it all works, and go on the defence–offence. It is often futile. Nowadays they get one warm but firm reply which challenges them to read all my books, listen to my podcasts (these are free, I might add) and then, and only then, come back with any question they have. Sometimes they do, and I admire that greatly and will help all I can. Sometimes they whinge that I am selling them something (which I get all of 30 pence net per book sale). These kind of emails, I can tell you, get ignored. (For a laugh I sometimes pass difficult or demanding enquiries on to my business partner, Mark. I know he's done the same to me!)

You can try, you can help, but you have to have a limit and a boundary at which point you say:

Oi.

You.

No.

When you start a new business or venture, you probably need to say yes a little more, as opportunities are more scarce. You want to open doors. As you get busier, more successful, with more demands on your time, you want and need to start to say no more. Be more picky. Rank opportunities in order of importance and priority.

To finish the chapter, here are some ways to say 'no' more easily:

- Say 'Yes, but not now'. Or 'Yes, but can we do it later or schedule it in once I am done.'
- Say 'So-and-so can help you better with this, why not ask them?'
- Never answer the phone or respond to an email, unless you are free and not in the middle of something important. Call or email them back at your convenience.
- Have a PA, VA or message filter to gatekeep, allowing only qualifying requests to reach you directly.
- Schedule specific times for specific tasks like meetings, calls, admin and giving back.

Remember the world reacts to how you teach it to behave towards you. Start to retrain it to give you the opportunities you want, and politely reject, delay or pass on to others the opportunities you don't want or can't handle at this time.

43
Giving more value

I believe it was Tony Robbins who said, 'The secret to living is giving.' When I was £50,000 in consumer debt and repaying loans I could barely afford, I wasn't sure I fully believed this. I didn't feel like I had anything to give.

Giving is twofold: giving to yourself and giving to others. When I was in debt, and had a very empty mindset, I was terrible at both. In this chapter, we'll explore both the selfish and selfless benefits of giving more.

The world depends on giving and receiving in equal measure. There's supply and demand, production and consumption, and it all relies on equilibrium. Too much production leads to a surplus and too much consumption leads to scarcity. It's the same at the micro level (you) as it is at the macro level (society, globally). It works on the ecological level, too: we take oxygen that the plants give and give carbon dioxide that the plants take.

To sustain the perfect equilibrium that is your self-worth, make sure that you give and receive value in equal measure. If you are good at receiving, you will receive more. That works for attracting everything from compliments to cash. If you are a great giver, you will also receive more, to balance the equilibrium and order of supply and demand. People give to a giver and take from a taker.

The 'Law of Reciprocity', according to Wikipedia, is a social norm of responding to a positive action with another positive action, rewarding kind actions. It's not what you get, it's what you get to give, and in giving you receive in equal measure.

Instead of saying 'I have to do this', instead say 'I get to do this'. To get more value, give more value. The more you give without the expectation of receiving, which could be construed as giving with an ulterior motive, the more you get in return.

Of course, this takes some faith, because you don't receive 'on demand'. There is a lag between your giving and receiving. You don't get to choose what exactly you receive and make a diary appointment with the universe on the date and time you receive it. But the more you keep giving, while simultaneously receiving the gifts, help and opportunities that come your way, most of what you want will come to you.

I find that giving boosts your self-worth battery life, because we are hardwired to be rewarded emotionally, proportionately to the level and scale of the giving. Good feelings increase self-worth. If there is anything to become addicted to, it is the feeling of giving. Give more and more, and get more and more hits of those feel-good chemicals.

I know that most people want to give more, both for selfish and selfless reasons. Often, we forget because we let menial tasks get in the way of meaningful ones. We can get ourselves into such a hole that we focus only on what we need. We can lose faith in the law of reciprocity because we feel unfairly treated, for example we help others and they don't help in return. Don't let these get in the way of the gift of giving more value. If at first you give for purely selfish reasons – that you will feel good, and that you need help in return – then that's still a good start. That's OK.

I find a great way to wrestle with my personal pain, with critics and with things that haven't gone my way is to get catharsis and therapy from giving. Here's how:

- Give such great value that your critics simply can't deny you.
- Productively and positively hone raw emotion and pain into value to pass on to others.
- What you have wrestled with, and how you solved it, can help others do the same.
- Helping others when you feel shit will make you feel immediately better.

My podcast is great for this. A blog or journal or writing a book, or creating an online course, can transfigure and repackage the criticism and pain you receive and feel, the perceived wrongs done to you, into something productive and of value to others. This obeys the law of conservation of energy: that energy can neither be created nor destroyed; rather, it can only be transformed from one form to another. You send the energy outwards instead of inwards. This creates a positive feedback loop for your self-worth. It feels good to be valuable. It feels even better to turn hardship and pain into something productive.

I like to compartmentalize a specific time in my day and diary purely for giving back, adding value and helping others. This way I know it gets done, but not to the detriment of what I feel I need to get done. It doesn't matter if it is 15 minutes a week, or 15 hours a week. It matters that you start, and that you do it on your terms and time, gratefully not in resentment that it's encroaching on your tasks. Here are some ideas:

- You could speak to people on the phone and simply listen.
- You could run an educational webinar that will reach many people.
- You could do voluntary work.

- You could donate money or set up your own foundation.
- You could turn your knowledge and experience into educational material.
- You could run apprenticeships or sponsor people.
- You could lecture and teach …

I could go on and on. You could turn your pain into value, the greatest leverage of the law of conservation of energy.

In Chapter 30 (Reverse comparison), I shared the pain that an amazing lady endured growing up. (You might like to look back to remind yourself of what she went through.)

This pain could have literally killed her. Instead, she *chose* to use and leverage it as a force for good. This is the rest of the story (radio edit):

- She was hired at a local black radio station to do the news part-time.
- She became the youngest news anchor and first black female news anchor.
- She signed a deal for her own show.
- She interviewed Michael Jackson, which became the third most watched interview ever.
- She started her own magazine (*O*) – the most successful start-up magazine in the industry.
- She became the first African American woman among America's 50 most generous people.
- She's given over $400 million to educational causes and funded more than 400 scholarships.
- She's got her own TV and media network which makes $300 million a year.
- She is worth around $3 billion.
- She now flies in her own $42-million, custom-designed Global Express XRS jet.

- She even has her own street: 'Oprah Winfrey Way' (so finally, if you haven't guessed long ago, I have given the game away).

Tom Cruise grew up in near poverty. The family was dominated by his abusive father, whom Cruise has described as 'a merchant of chaos'. He was beaten by his father, who Cruise has said was 'a bully and coward'. He was the kind of person who, if something goes wrong, kicks you. Tom has gone on to educate and entertain hundreds of millions of people.

Victor Frankl was imprisoned at several concentration camps by Nazis, including at Auschwitz. His wife and family were killed by the Nazis. He used this pain and wrote the amazing book *Man's Search for Meaning*, one of 'the ten most influential books in the United States'. At the time of his death in 1997, the book had sold over 10 million copies and had been translated into 24 languages.

J. K. Rowling experienced failure, rejection, domestic abuse and divorce. She became clinically depressed. These were the real nightmares for this out-of-work single mother living on welfare and contemplating suicide. Twenty publishers rejected her manuscript of *Harry Potter and the Philosopher's Stone*. She saw herself as 'the biggest failure' she knew, yet she turned her despair into her inspiration. Her persistence of never giving up enabled her from going from broke, jobless and living on welfare to a multimillionaire in less than five years. She is apparently richer than the queen with an estimated wealth of £500 million.

We aren't all going to reach these heights, and by now you should realize that one of the cardinal rules is that we shouldn't compare ourselves to anyone else. But we can be inspired, and we can use these examples of how pain and hardship can be transmuted into giving more value.

44

Putting yourself out there (more)

You don't need a load of rah-rah, whoop-whoop hell-yeahs from me to know that most people, including you, know what to do. You just need to bloody go and do it.

If you had a shop, you could be the best cashier or salesperson in the world and you could win awards for the best-dressed shop window. But if you didn't get anyone in the shop, you'd have no shop, because you'd have no one to sell to. You wouldn't be able to pay your rent. You'd go bust.

I know for a fact that you have a unique set of skills and talents. I know you do what you do really well. I know you could be the very best. But the world won't know that until you start putting yourself out there more.

I used to be an artist. My strategy and reaction to not selling my paintings was to paint more. That's like eating more if you're not losing weight. I didn't need more paintings that no one would see and no one would buy. I needed to sell the ones I'd already done. There was nothing wrong with them. The reality was that not enough people were seeing my pieces. I didn't get my paintings out to more galleries. I didn't get my paintings out of Peterborough, FFS. I didn't approach agents and dealers with my work. I didn't get more traffic to my website. To be honest, I didn't really get out of my studio/house/cave/hole that I lived in.

Sometimes you just need to have a good word with yourself. Give yourself a stern talking to, a little slap maybe, and get yourself out there more. You're not an introvert (remember Chapter 29?). You have nothing to be afraid of. Post more on social media. Get out to events. Get on the phone and talk to people. Do livestreams and webinars. Go to parties and functions that you'd usually turn down. Go to reunions.

Here are some practical ways to put yourself out there more (and they're not just for introverts):

- *Stop overthinking it and start testing it.* Don't waste precious time worrying and overthinking about whether you'll mess up, be judged or that you won't be good enough. Instead, just got for it. Prepare, to a point, but then just do it.
- *Remember that everything is a test.* Nothing, including you, ever has to be the perfect finished final product. If something turns out bad, you can always go back and fix it. Stop making it seem so big and permanent in your mind. Understand how small your actions are in the grand scheme of things and take that pressure off yourself.
- *Ask yourself, 'What's the worst that could happen?'* What is the absolute worst-case scenario for putting yourself, your content, your products, services and even soul out into the world? It's not death. It's not disownment. People might not like it or you. If that happens, which is unlikely, you can learn from it and move on. Thank them and move on.
- *Ask yourself, "What will happen if I don't?'* Think about what you'll miss out on if you don't put yourself out there. Think of all the things that might not happen for you. Think of all the opportunities you may miss. The competitors you may lose to. The people you'll never meet. The lovers. Followers. Fans. Clients. Think

about where you will be ten years down the line if
you stay too scared to move forward, or too hidden
away to be seen by anyone.

- *Remember that you can always 'press the delete button'.*
  If you really don't like something you've put out, or
  afterwards feel like you could have done better, then
  just 'delete' it. But first, you have to put it out there
  and give it a chance. You might even end up surprised
  at the results and be glad you chose not to delete it. If
  'it' can't be deleted, because it is something you said
  or did that you can't take back, you can still delete it
  from your mind. Or know that in five minutes or a
  week whoever it was would have forgotten about it.
  Better sometimes to beg for forgiveness than to seek
  permission.

- *Get some (more) accountability.* Get a failsafe in place
  that forces you to be accountable and follow through
  with your plans. Feel personally responsible if you
  fail to put yourself or your work out there. Whether
  it's a coach or a mentor, a bet or a competition, a
  community or accountability group, or making public
  commitment posts on social media that force you into
  accountability.

- *Start with something you know well.* If you're not sure
  where to begin, or your fears and self-worth issues are
  getting the better of you, start with something you
  know really well. A chosen niche. An area of interest
  or experience. Build your confidence up with things
  you are unshakeable on, then scale up from there.

- *Know that you have something unique to share (you are
  you, after all).* Don't limit yourself or keep your voice
  and ideas from being heard, just because you think

there are other people saying or doing things better than you. They can't say or do them the way you can, because there's no one else in the whole world like you. There's space in your niche for you. There's always room at the top. There are plenty of authors, entrepreneurs and influencers, but here we are, attracted to each other somehow.

- *Stop playing small. Stop overthinking it. Start putting yourself out there (more).*

45
Your go-to, three-step, triple-A self-worth system

In Chapter 5 (How we value anything and everything) and Chapter 11 (Self-doubt), I shared a simple three-step, triple-A system for managing and then mastering your self-worth:

1 **(Be) aware:** Gain awareness, and then mastery, of your emotions.
2 **Accept:** It is how it is meant to be. You can't change it. Discover new facts about yourself that you're not yet seeing that help you accept this.
3 **Act:** See balance in any situation (the upside to the downside, or vice versa). Then do something positive and proactive about it.

This system works in all areas that affect your self-worth negatively. Here's a little more detail to help you implement the three-step system:

1. (Be) aware

Gain awareness, and then mastery, of your emotions.

First, notice the emotions. We have a unique ability as human beings to be aware of our emotions. We are able to separate ourselves from our emotions, become conscious of them, and evaluate them in real time. That's quite an amazing skill you have that you can probably leverage much more than you are doing now.

I like to think of it as splitting my mind or consciousness into two parts – even two people, or voices, inside my own head. One is the emotion I am feeling. It is likely to be strong and sending chemicals all around my body. The other is more passive – an onlooker that observes, noticing and commenting on that emotion.

Let's say I get a one-star review, or my wife is 'really tired and wants an early night', or the kids are pounding each other at four in the morning. The initial raw emotion fires off automatically. It could be frustration, anger or rejection. Then it builds. Then all the past situations and baggage dump themselves on top and build it further. Then …

Stop.

Wait.

Observe and disconnect.

Do not punch anyone (just yet).

Then on to step 2 …

2. Accept

It is how it is meant to be. You can't change it. Discover new facts about yourself that you're not yet seeing that help you accept this.

You can jump up and down all you want. You can spray a load of wasted energy all over the place, but it won't change a thing. Stop wishing it were different. It is what it is. It is what it is supposed to be, not what you wish it to be.

Now search for the facts that exist, hidden in plain sight, clouded by raw emotion, that you are not seeing, or are seeing in an unbalanced way. The past is gone. The baggage has nothing to do with the present predicament. Don't let it affect the reality. This is a first-world problem. I make a choice about how I let situations affect me. I have control over my emotions. They are not intending to make me feel this way. Why am I feeling this way and what am I supposed to learn from this situation?

3. Act

See balance in any situation (the upside to the downside, or vice versa). Then do something positive and proactive about it.

Put this into context and look at the situation in an alternative or positive perspective. What gifts does this situation bring?

Can I learn valuable feedback from the one-star reviews? Does it make the other reviews look more credible, as they're not all five-star ones? Will I be humbled and grounded so that I continue to offer value and improve? Do I have a lot of work to do so getting up at 4am would actually work to my advantage? Is this an opportunity to have a play-fight rough and tumble with the kids? Might it wake the wife and might she fancy the cuddle we didn't have the night before ... Am I now dreaming? Do these challenges help me deal with these and bigger situations better next time?

Then make a clear, proactive decision. How are you going to solve this? What next steps are you taking to move towards a resolution?

No matter how big or small the challenge is, you can teach yourself this 'triple-A' process. The good news is you get to practise it each time the world throws a challenge at you, so the bigger your challenges, the better you get at mastering them.

I used to be unaware that this could even be done, because I was always a victim to, and being controlled by, my emotions. Once I learned you don't need to be controlled by them, this process would sometimes take me days, instead of weeks. Each time you get to practise it, you can shorten the time it takes to get through the stages, such that in some situations you could go through the whole process in one second or less, automatically as part of the emotional reaction.

I have found that letting go, not being so stubborn, not holding a grudge or having to be right all the time have really helped in managing my emotions more effectively. Add forgiveness of yourself and others, and not taking things personally to this list, and you are likely to be generally more happy and productive and have a deeper, stronger, more unshakeable sense of self-worth.

Managing and mastering your emotions

46

The tricks your emotions play on you

Woven throughout Parts 2 to 4 are proactive steps you can take towards having a stronger self-worth. Part 5 will add to this, focusing on strategies and tactics that will help you manage and master your emotions.

I believe managing your emotions to be one of the key holistic life skills. There was a time, basically my whole life before 2006, when I had no awareness that you could actually 'manage' your emotions. I was never taught this. While my dad instilled in me a belief that I could achieve anything I put my mind to, it didn't equip me to deal with the greatest challenge of all that life throws at us: not what happens to us, but how we react to it.

Your business can grow only at the speed that you grow. Your relationships and friendships – professional, personal and intimate – are a reflection of you and how you treat others, how you channel your emotions in their service. Your money will only grow if you can manage the emotions that grow or erode wealth. Your eating habits and fitness are largely dictated by your emotions. And possibly most important of all, your relationship with yourself and your self-worth.

Every human being experiences every human emotion, providing they have full mental health and capacity. You are no worse than anyone else because you feel or wrestle with certain emotions. In fact, you are not your emotions at all; your emotions are fleeting feelings, you are greater than every one of them. Emotions are simply personal, internal feedback systems to help you survive, grow and thrive independently and interdependently. They serve to help you react to your environment, threats and opportunities.

They do play tricks on you though, and that's the subject of this chapter.

Separating who you are from the emotions you feel in the moment helps you gain more clarity about your true identity. It helps you to make wise decisions that serve you. If the upside of your emotions is that they serve as valuable feedback for your ongoing growth, the downside is that they play tricks on you. You can be quickly lured into focusing on how you feel, rather than remembering who you are.

You are not a coiled-up spring of frustration and impatience. You are not insignificant and unworthy. You are not an angry bastard. You are not twisted with jealousy and hate. But you may feel like this from time to time. These emotions are strong. They need to be strong. They need to be stronger than your positive emotions, because they need to alert you to imminent threats. You need to be interrupted in the middle of your routines so you can save yourself from danger.

A heightened emotion in the moment will dissipate soon enough, but you are with yourself your whole life, and you will encounter those emotions again so must have a strategy for dealing with them when they arise. Therefore, be very alert to the tricks your emotions play on you. These include:

- making things appear worse (or harder) than they really are
- making things appear better (or easier) than they really are
- forcing you to be reactive rather than proactive
- forcing you to be fearful rather than faithful
- making you question your actions or identity in an unreasonable way

- forcing short-term decisions due to a current feeling
- bringing up past emotions that affect current and future decisions adversely
- deceiving you into taking up an extreme or one-side stance
- allowing even unrelated things to be affected by how you feel in the moment.

If you follow the 'triple-A' system – Aware, Accept, Act – then you can transcend and survive an emotional onslaught without making any rash, volatile decisions (good or bad). This goes for emotional eating, emotional spending, borrowing and lending, sending emails, debates-turned-arguments, punishment of yourself and others, relationships you engage in, hiring, firing, investing … everything.

Do your best not to make (m)any decisions when experiencing strong or extreme emotions. You will make most of your *bad* decisions under the duress of your emotions, like when David (or Bruce) Banner turns into the Hulk and back again.

Don't send that email when you are really angry with what you have just read. Don't lash out and say hurtful things when you feel hurt by others. Don't eat when you feel lonely, rejected or depressed. Don't go on a shopping spree when you are feeling ecstatic. Don't take your bad day out on your kids. Don't respond to your haters when they lure you into an online 'debate'. Don't get distracted from your main task when the desire to procrastinate kicks in (note to self as I write this book).

Your emotions will create a compelling case (and lots of pain) to egg you on to unleash all hell and fury on someone. You don't just dump your current emotion all over them; you unleash your entire life on them. You don't need me to tell you that when you've done that (and you know when you've done that), you have most likely regretted it. It has put you right in the shit. You have squandered opportunities or shot yourself in the face or had to eat humble pie and apologize, like a puppy that's pissed the carpet.

Just wait. Sit on your hands, shut your mouth and ride it out. Tomorrow, or in an hour, you will feel very different.

Only kids do everything based on how they feel in the moment. They don't have the benefit of experience of the consequences of their tantrums. You do.

And you shouldn't always trust your emotions in the first place. They can overreact. They can generalize. They can take situations way out of context. They can be childish. They don't have all the evidence. Just because something feels really good, or really bad to you doesn't mean it is at all.

People say you should 'trust your feelings' and 'identify with your emotions'. I wouldn't trust people who say that! Your feelings can fool you and rule you. Your intuition is often wrong – after all, you don't know what you don't know. Question your emotions. Be sceptical of what they are trying to get you to do. Then, trust them.

As I am writing this, on the train from London, a guy is sitting right opposite me is eating a Pret mac and cheese. He is chomping away, showing me the entire contents of his mouth. He's only eating one bite at a time, waiting 30 seconds and then taking another slow bite. He's been eating it since 1985, clearly just to piss me off. I really, really want to pick up the box and chuck it in the bin.

At exactly the same time, the train manager is talking over the Tannoy like she's in a helicopter. She is reeling off more information than Google stores in its data centres. I really, really want to get hold of the microphone, tear it from its cable, and throw it out of the window. Don't they know I'm writing my book? I am imagining all this in great detail. My arms are getting tense and feel acidic.

Well, of course, I didn't act on those emotions and I'm not in prison. Everything about me wanted to do this for a few minutes. For a minute there, I lost myself.

A strong emotion that has the effect of creating a temporary sense of self-worth is the need to be right all the time. If you have endured a few cycles of this, you will know that you may very well be right, but no one says, 'Thank you for showing me the way. You are right, oh holy and wise one. I needed you to shoot me down in front of everyone to realize the error of my ways.' If you are right, they are pissed off. How does that serve you exactly? Well, you get the short-term fix of feeling impor-tant. Then you have the comedown.

Now that man is eating a massive bag of Tyrrell's crisps. They are the crunchiest crisps ever cooked in the history of the world. Really? Give. Me. Strength.

Anyway, to summarize this chapter:

- Don't confuse your fleeting emotions with your inner self-worth.
- Don't let your inner child make rash, emotional decisions.
- Make important decisions when the emotion subsides and you are more balanced.
- Question your emotions before you act upon them.
- Learn the implications of emotional decisions in the past, and use that as feedback for the present and future.

Arguments in your head aren't real, but they sure can feel like it at the time. Beware those pesky emotions and the tricks they play on you. They come out of nowhere and blindside you. Be ready. Stay vigilant.

Now he's on his phone. In the quiet coach, where I spe-cifically sat in to get some peace and quiet to write this book. WTAF.

47
When you know you should
know better

I have this beating myself up for beating myself up pattern I play to myself sometimes. Like it's not enough for me to beat myself up; I then beat myself up for beating myself up. And then I feel I should know better than to do that so I beat myself up some more.

And having read or listened to many thousands of personal development and business books, attended courses and had many mentors, and all that money invested in the last decade, I really should know better than to make some of the silly mistakes I make.

Feeling like I should know better serves to remind me not to do it again. But I still do. More often, however, it just makes me feel like I am a slow learner and a bit of an idiot for not putting into action what I learned, and struggling to practise what I preach.

I am the author of this book but still experience regular challenges to my self-worth. I'm on the train back to London, having just met the billionaire Sir Tom Hunter. I was very nervous before I met him, and started to internally pick at myself. 'You're not worthy. What if he doesn't like me?' I should know better than this. I should read my own book. Hmmm.

It wasn't a conscious thing. As I was going up in the lift I had a little word with myself, or three words in fact: Aware. Accept. Act. I talked myself up and mostly got over myself. Sir Tom was lovely, as pretty much all the successful and super-rich people

I've met are. Yet I still have these nerves and inner voices and there they go, peck-peck-peck at my self-worth.

You can hear our conversation on my 'Disruptive Entrepreneur' podcast, where we talk about this feeling meeting new and successful people, and his business and philanthropic ventures. He had no idea what I was thinking, feeling and saying to myself in my head. In fact, he was quite surprised when I told him. This is worth remembering: all the things we are thinking, and feeling, and worrying about, and second-guessing, and doubting … well, other people aren't aware of them. It is highly unlikely that they are thinking the same things about us that we are thinking about ourselves. They may well have their own voices in their head. They are likely far more positive about us than we are about ourselves. Remember:

- We are all a work in progress.
- We are all doing the best we can with what we know.
- We all have self-worth challenges that throw themselves at us consistently.
- Just because you should know better doesn't mean you are more of a failure.
- Just because you continue to make mistakes you've made before, doesn't make you any less worthy.

They say: don't make the same mistake twice. They say: learn from your mistakes. That's good advice on paper, yet it's totally divorced from the real world. Everyone makes the same mistakes twice, five times, or over and over. This is because we are who we are: we are good at what we are good at, and bad at what we are bad at. We should know better than to make the same mistakes over and over, but we still do. It's who we are. As long as we have good intentions, it's OK. The best you can is good enough.

At one point in my personal development journey, I started to feel like I was one of those 'course junkies' that people refer to. The one who chases the 'shiny penny'. The one who actually does nothing but 'shelf development'. The one who is looking for the new thing to save him from the last thing he didn't give long enough to work. I felt like I was doing so much learning, and not enough doing. Then I would beat myself up about that and start to question everything.

Then one of my many mentors said to me: 'Rob, you never lose what you learn. It stays with you, and when the opportunities arise related to what you have learned, you will spot them. You will be ready when you are ready. Have faith in yourself.'

I have since learned that beating yourself up and feeling like you should know better simply makes you more tense, and less open to opportunities. If your brain is all tight like a dried-up walnut, you won't be able to use it to its full capacity. Stress will reduce your creativity as it will make you focus only on the threat or source of stress, and not on the solution or opportunity.

Instead of feeling like I needed to stop learning, and then implement what I last learned, heaping a whole load of pressure and tension on myself, I just kept learning. Of course, there is a time for doing, too, and both should be scheduled in your weekly diary. As an example of this, I am running an advanced speaking and selling course for my top trainers this week, and I have been able to draw on all the speaking and sales material I studied and invested in over the last decade. I may have felt at the time that I was learning more than doing, but it is still all there in the bank waiting to be cashed in. And so is everything you ever learn: it all goes into your experience bank and builds on your 'natural', innate intuition, which in turn helps you make faster and better decisions.

48
Self-awareness and knowledge

I'm often asked what are the biggest lessons I have learned in business/making money/life/parenting. I don't perceive myself as an all-knowing expert in these areas, but there's one answer that encompasses all the other possible answers: you can't manage or master any external situation if you can't manage and master your (inner) self. You won't get more money, time, freedom and happiness until you learn to manage what you already have. Socrates said, 'to know thyself is the beginning of wisdom'. Self-awareness and knowledge come from knowing:

- the lies you tell yourself (about letting yourself off the hook, about how you aren't good enough, etc.)
- when your emotions are playing tricks on you (emotional duress driving short-term decisions, emotional volatility and extremes)
- when you are bringing past emotional baggage into present decisions
- that you will feel different when the emotion has subsided
- the patterns you repeat and the consistent mistakes you make
- your great traits and your flaws equally
- the importance of continued investment in building your knowledge, awareness and experience
- how you influence and make others feel

- how to trick and second-guess yourself into action and progress
- your values, identity, personal moral code and what you will accept and reject
- how to centre and balance yourself when you experience extremes
- how to manage and contextualize your fears and significant painful/emotional events.

We spend so much time learning about other things and people, yet there is not as much focus on learning about ourselves. None of the above were taught in any school or university I ever went to. This means you can't expect the world to teach you about yourself, other than the hard knocks on-the-street lessons. You have to teach yourself. Traditional education will make you a living; self-education may make you a life.

Have a clear vision of who you are. Know who you want to become. Know how you want to be known by others. Commit to a path of constant and never-ending education, development and embracing feedback.

Aware. Accept. Act.

Maintain a balanced outlook. Each time you get overly emotional, volatile or one-sided, remind yourself of the polar perspective. Give yourself the right inner counsel, and don't allow it to become an inner critic. Get the wise counsel of others, and have the wisdom to know when you need help or you're getting in your own way. Here are some practical things you can do to continually develop and master your self-awareness and knowledge:

- Get great mentors and smart people to pick, lift and drag you up.
- Keep reading and listening to books, audiobooks, podcasts and great influencers.

- Attend courses, seminars, masterclasses and online programmes.
- Join a mastermind group or proactive network in your passion and profession.
- Watch autobiographical and educational documentaries.
- Join forums and online community groups in your chosen niches.

And here are some ideas for critical thinking you can practise to continue the road of constant and never-ending self-improvement:

- Generally accept what you can't control.
- Take full and final responsibility of what you can.
- Never blame, complain, defend or justify; instead, serve and solve.
- Do not believe either your own hype or your low self-worth, in equal measure.
- External validation does not make any difference to who you are.
- Question everything, including your inner voice, with a solution focus.
- Own your successes and failures equally.

There are many talented people and failed geniuses who had everything going for them, but lacked the self-awareness to maintain balance, humility and a continual development mind set. There are people who literally self-sabotage much of the great things about their life, because of an internal struggle they have. Conversely, there are others who aren't viewed as talented or special, but who got to know themselves (and their limitations) well and committed to self-development.

The best English cricket batsman of all time is not the best batsman of all time. Graham Gooch, Kevin Pietersen, David

Gower and many others had all the repertoire of shots, flair and apparent natural talent. While these are all greats of the game, none scored anywhere near as many runs as Alistair Cook. Yes, I know I've lauded his achievements earlier in the book, but he's worth mentioning again in this context. Cook knew his abilities, and he knew he didn't have the apparent gifts the other batsmen did. He played within himself, focused on two main strokes, despite others having all the shots, and ground out the runs and the centuries over a long career. He consistently maintained humility, fitness and desire to improve his game. Even after a dip at the end of his career, he went out on his last test match scoring a 70 and a century in his final test, and wrote himself into the history books more than any other English batsman.

If you make money, you can just as easily lose it, but once you have learned something of value, you can't unlearn it. It stays with you as an asset for as long as you live, continually feeding back into and improving other areas of your life.

And so I say, 'You are your best asset, you pay yourself the best interest, invest in yourself wisely.'

And one final thing, don't take yourself too seriously all the time. Stay light, approachable and fun. Be someone whom others love to be around. We can get so consumed by our first-world problems and spend so much time trying to make a living that we forget to really live a life.

49
Balanced expectations

I guess you've figured out by now that I believe there to be an upside in every perceived downside, and a downside in every perceived upside. I believe there to be a balanced paradox in everything that exists. This paradox can be perceived as a contradiction, and this is especially apparent when it comes to expectations.

Here are a couple of famous quotes that together encapsulate the paradox of expectations:

'Shoot for the moon. Even if you miss, you'll land among the stars.'

Norman Vincent Peale

'My expectations were reduced to zero when I was 21. Everything since then has been a bonus.'

Stephen Hawking

Which one is correct? Should you manage and reduce your expectations so that you are not disappointed or demotivated? Or should you set big goals and expectations, so that, even if you never reach them, you'd still be well on your way to success?

And then there is Roosevelt's quote I shared earlier: 'Comparison is the thief of joy.'

Should you accept all that happens to you, as a way of being spiritual and happy? Or should you work and chase and hustle for the things that you want and not accept it how it is. To not take no for an answer?

If two people are having a dispute, and you're stuck in the middle as the go-between mediator, it's likely that you will get two unbalanced, extremely one-sided viewpoints. Both sides are convinced they are right, and the other side is wrong. But that can't be possible.

When it comes to expectations, the most empowering, consistent and enduring outcomes arise from a balance between the paradoxical extremes:

- Accept what is, but strive for more.
- Set a (big) goal, but enjoy the journey too.
- Be grateful despite things being hard.
- Expect nothing but try for everything.
- Make things happen and let things happen.
- Be focused on the money, but don't be all about the money.
- Be and do.
- Trust but verify.
- Strive for more and celebrate what you've done.
- Think BIG, start small.
- Meditate and manifest, then uncross your legs and get shit done.

Social and mainstream media aren't geared up to helping you maintain balanced expectations and perspectives. It's mostly extreme, one-sided, controversial content that gets headlines and attention. Be careful what you get lured into believing through these media channels and the one-sided clickbait.

Wisdom and longevity lie in the balancing of polarized forces that pull against each other. Expect everything *and* nothing. Struggle *and* let go. Demand *and* accept. All simultaneously if possible.

Even balance is a paradox: strive for balance knowing you may never achieve balance. Balance itself, like a seesaw, is rarely in perfect equilibrium. Even when no one is sitting on a seesaw, it is one side up and one side down. Even when two people sit on it, it swings from one side up to the other. A seesaw in action constantly moves across the full range, from one extreme to the other.

I both love and hate writing books. I get overwhelmed, then bored. I'm frustrated, then motivated. All these things and others wrestle with one other and create a tension that oscillates between order and chaos. Even when we perceive we want order, we need chaos, and vice versa. Our struggles determine our successes.

What are you willing to struggle for? What pain are you willing to accept? Let go of the fantasy of one-sidedness, and dance with the paradox of expectations. Expect nothing. Demand everything. Enjoy the journey *and* focus on the goal. Know you are worth everything now, *and* strive to become more and better. Love the person that you are, *and* have a vision of who you want to become.

50
Love and gratitude

To my knowledge, it is impossible to be both grateful and resentful in the same moment in time. I was going to say you can't both love and hate in the same moment, but if you are married or have kids you might feel differently.

I believe the antidote to all suffering is love and gratitude. They are the purest of emotions. One of my mentors, Dr John Demartini, says that 'gratitude and love are the only two pure, transcendent human emotions'. I'm still trying to figure out the true depth of what that really means, but no matter how big your challenges, problems and pains, they immediately dissipate when you allow yourself to feel gratitude and love. You immediately shift focus from what you lack to what you have, and what is a curse to what is a gift. Counting your blessings cures your fears and failures.

The reason you don't put your kids up for adoption every time they have a meltdown is because, despite all the challenges they throw at you, you never doubt or question your love for them. You give them the benefit of the doubt because you know they are learning to manage their own emotions. You know they are beautiful little people. If we can carry this attitude to other people in our lives, and to situations that challenge us, then we can transcend anxiety, stress, anger, hate – all emotions that damage our self-worth.

With love and gratitude, you are enough, and everyone else is enough. Everything is just as it should be, not as you wish it would be.

Love and gratitude connect us together. The oxytocin in our system is triggered by acts such as giving thanks and appreciation. These trigger pro-social behaviours such as trust, generosity and affection.

To '*count* your blessings', '*practise* gratitude' and '*give* thanks' contain verbs (action words), and love and gratitude aren't just emotions that happen *to* you – you (can) *do* them and practise them. You improve your ability to do and feel them. You get them more frequently as a reward for developing the skill and ability.

This is where I believe meditation, mindfulness, presence and spiritual outlook really come into their own. These practices can give you a better skill set of creating and feeling more love and gratitude. They can create empowering habits and the ability to react more positively and productively to challenging situations, and to control the stress hormones that are triggered by all the threats around us.

Of course, it isn't always going to be easy. Just when you feel in control of your reactions to the circumstances around you, something really hard happens. Or you get blindsided by something that shocks you. Or the one thing that really gets under your skin keeps showing up like a monkey on your back that you can't shake off. But it's in these moments of challenge and hardship that you really get to practise love and gratitude for real, because anyone can do it when life is easy.

Practise seeing the world from the other person's point of view, to help you understand and be compassionate to where they are at. Practise being grateful when things go well, rather than moving on too quickly, or feeling as if you don't deserve it. Practise gratitude when things don't go your way. You can be grateful in all situations, if you practise it:

- Be grateful for the good in the bad.
- Be grateful that things aren't much worse (because they always could be).
- Be grateful that you get to grow.
- Be grateful that you are big enough and ready enough for the current challenge.
- Be grateful that the timing could be worse.
- Be grateful that you get to both protect and show others the way to deal with the challenge.
- Be grateful that this challenge will draw the right people to you, for a deeper connection.

Love and gratitude are the cure-all antidote to all feelings of low self-worth. You have the power within you and the antidote in your hands; you just need to choose to use it. Practise gratitude daily. I like to run over all the things I am grateful for, in my head before bed. Also, try to catch things during the day that you are grateful for – both small things and all things. The more you do it the more you feel it.

Gratitude leads to more love. Love in a centred, poised sense, not an infatuated sense or soppy sense. Love leads to certainty, presence, inspiration, purpose, power, vitality, clarity and freedom. Which leads to more gratitude, which transcends all self-worth-related issues instantly.

Oh and yes, practise loving yourself, too.

51

What goes in must come out

I can be an angry bastard. I can get wildly jealous. I've felt the desire to reject people who've rejected me and hurt people who've hurt me. Have this #Fuckers.

But I am also non-confrontational. I don't want to upset people in any way. I don't want any conflict. I'm soft. I want them to like me. Please like me/love me.

In the past things would get under my skin, likely on a daily basis, and then build and build and build. I'd want to let it all out, but didn't have the courage, so I'd hold it in. But anything that has a build-up of pressure also has to have an outlet valve somewhere. I didn't. When there is no outlet valve, the pressure builds up until finally there is a great big massive sonic-boom explosion.

That great big massive sonic-boom explosion would happen to me about twice a year. My feelings were totally out of control. I might threaten to beat up all my friends in a fit of rage (though I never did so). I might kick or punch a door or wall and cut or break my knuckles or metatarsals. I might smash the living shit out of anything in my vicinity (lamps, laptops, Walk-mans, phones, golf bags – they've all taken a huge beating from me). I might shout and scream and wail. I might do all three at once. This was my curse until I was 25 years old.

While this felt necessary at the time – I had to get rid of that pressure – it was unhealthy. It was an instance of the law of conservation of energy – inside me. I was allowing it to build and form into anger. The flip-out release would come,

I would create and cause chaos all around me, then, when the dust settled, the guilt would kick in. Hard. And then the cycle would slowly begin again. I just put this down to me having occasional anger issues, as something I would have to accept and live with. Had I not addressed it, however, it could have continued to escalate to the point where I did something really bad to myself or someone I cared about.

Before I share some lessons and methods to release your own strong (especially negative) emotions, safely and quietly, it's OK to admit that, from time to time:

- your husband/wife/partner can really fuckin' piss you off
- your children can drive you crazy
- your friends and colleagues can be massive dicks
- your customers can complain like little childish twats ...

In general, it can seem that people are put on this earth just to fuck you off constantly.

I used to try to deny this. People are kind, aren't they? You should always see the good in people, shouldn't you? People are doing the best they can, aren't they? They don't mean to upset you, do they? See it from their perspective ...

Yes, maybe, but they still piss you off.

To save you from screaming in their face, there are two stages to what you can do before you do something really silly under strong emotional duress:

- Stage 1: Stop yourself from doing or saying something silly by substituting a replacement behaviour/response.
- Stage 2: Engineer a cathartic release to relieve the emotion and stop the build-up–break stuff pattern (leverage the law of conservation of energy outward).

Here are some methods for tackling Stage 1:

- Learn to smile even if it's hard to do. Listen, observe, even thank them.
- Try to understand they may be dealing with their own difficulties and emotions.
- Stay quiet. Say nothing. Do nothing. Do not reply to the email. Do not retaliate.
- Let people talk, rant and burn their emotion out. Often, they will calm down.
- Care about them. Have a desire to fix and solve the problem.
- Be grateful that you can control your response and act on it measuredly.
- And, in more extreme cases, just walk away from the situation.

Give yourself some time to calm down and regain your composure. Let the emotion subside so you can gain some clarity, balance and logic. Sometimes a little time to breathe or think things through is all you actually need to release the pressure of the emotion and the situation. At other times, to stop the exponential build-up, try one of the following, which can be helpful for implementing stage 2:

- Have a friend you trust whom you can rant to.
- Have trusted, wise counsellors or mentors who can advise and balance you.
- Write or journal about how you feel (perhaps a private diary or a public blog)
- Have a creative release (music, art, YouTubing, podcasting, etc.).
- Have a physical release (fitness, martial arts, climbing, etc.).

People often ask me how I manage to get so many books, podcasts and general online content out. I've never really been able to answer this until recently. I just thought that it was something I did, and that it was normal and easy. But now I've had a rethink. The real reason, I think, is because I'm just a bit screwed up! My podcasts, books, blogs, articles, live videos and rants have been therapy for me. Much of what I 'bottle up' (wanting to flip out on the inside but at the same time wanting to maintain some dignity and respect on the outside) gets to come out via my writing, sharing and teaching. And especially my ranting. It is a very healthy, cathartic exercise for me. It also helps others and builds my brand. This in turn gives me good external proof that feeds back into and increases my self-worth.

There is no reason why you can't do the same. Find your creative, physical and cathartic release. Can you take those strong, inward emotions and direct them out onto and into the world in the cause of good? The pain you feel, can you use it to help and inspire others?

Think about it: if you hold it in, it will either come out in a way you aren't in control of or, worse, cause stress, depression or disease. That in turn will erode your self-worth further. Instead, hone the powerful negative energy and put it out into something useful and meaningful, like J. K. Rowling, Oprah and Tom Cruise have (see Chapter 43).

One final thing, I don't ever regret keeping my mouth shut and smiling, but I can recount many a time when I regretted opening my mouth and lashing out. There's a lot to be said for a silent smile. Grace under pressure. Hold that smile. Walk away. Then get your release somewhere more productive and positive.

52
Ask for help. Please

I'm perplexed why so many people feel that asking for help is a weakness. Perhaps we don't want to be viewed as vulnerable? Perhaps we are too proud and our ego gets in the way? Perhaps we want to maintain a perfect (if false) image of ourselves? Perhaps we feel social pressure to be positive and resilient?

We all struggle. We all feel lost. We all rely on each other for support and survival. As a species we flourish on interdependence and interaction. To survive and evolve we are helping one other all the time. So why is asking for help, especially when you actually need it, any different from what we are already doing – in the background, so to speak?

I used to expect my wife to intuitively know everything that I wanted. As if she could read my mind or something. I would never ask, probably for fear of rejection or expectation, but sit and wait and hope and expect that she could read my mind and fulfil all my desires. Funnily enough, she wasn't well versed in telepathy (she really does need to work on these skills, though I won't be passing on that feedback to her!).

Asking for help has many practical benefits. I'm going to list them out. They are clear, obvious and practical. Practise asking more for help, especially when you need it the most. Do not suffer alone. Someone can help. People want to help:

- If you don't ask for help, they don't know that you need help, and are not able to help.
- It is a quicker and easier way to solve your problem.

- People love to help, so you give them a gift by asking for help.
- You need a fresh perspective: it can take someone else's input to solve a problem you created.
- It teaches you humility and a desire to learn – a great pair of life skills.
- It will inspire others who are struggling to reach out and ask for help, too.

I used to think that the smartest people never needed to ask for help. I was wrong. It is the complete opposite in my new opinion. The smartest people ask for help. Mentors don't just mentor; they have mentors and ask for help, too. It is a strength not a weakness. Be strong. Reach out.

If you're ever really struggling, ask for help. If things are really bad, seek professional help. My dad hates seeing doctors, but it doesn't make him weak if he has an issue and only a professional can help fix it. This is as important for your mental health as it is your physical health. If you Google 'help with depression' or 'help with suicidal thoughts' there are many great organizations who can be on instant telephone support. If things are bad, but not *that* bad, reach out to me. Message me on one of my social media platforms (search Rob Moore or Rob Moore Progressive), and if I can help, I will do my best to be there for you. I've also done podcasts and YouTube videos on dealing with depression (mostly, admittedly, with entrepreneurs in mind) and they have had good feedback. Look them up or share them with someone you know who is struggling and just needs a helping hand. You are not alone – never forget that.

Ask for help.

53
When. Is. It. Ever. Enough?

You want to strive for more, but you'd also like to be happy now. You need the hunger and impatience and sense of account- ability to drive you, but that's also frustrating and chaotic and hard. You want to grow into something, hope it will be bigger, better, more, but you also want to soak up and appreciate what you have already achieved now. You want to become a better person, but also be happy with who you already are.

The trouble is, that doesn't make for a good soundbite on social media. You're told by everyone to either:

Hustle and grind, 24/7/365, #no lunch #no days off #100- hour weeks

Or …

Accept all that is. Just 'be'. Meditate and manifest happiness. Be grateful and present in the moment.

So, which one is right? Well, neither and both.

While 'it' may never be 'enough', you *are* enough. You are worth everything you desire. You have so much to be grateful for and happy about. You have nothing to prove. Things are exactly as they should be.

And you want to be, do and have more. And then when you do, you will want to be, do and have more. And when you do, so it will continue. And that's exactly how it should be, too. Progress towards a worthy goal equals happiness.

If it weren't for our insecurities, guilt, low self-worth, frustration – all those void emotions we feel in our lives – we would have nothing to fill/fulfil. We wouldn't drive and strive for more. There would be no solutions, service or progress. Our values are linked to our voids: we seek to fill/fulfil what we lack, to fill what is empty, which forces us to grow, achieve and self-actualize. Sometimes those voids are filled, and that feels good, but the progress stops. If we fulfil a value, it simply changes form and a new void opens up.

- Maybe you get out of debt, but as soon as that void and pain disappears you start spending and get lured back in again.
- Maybe when you are single you are down the gym twice a day, ripped and lean, but then when you get comfortable in a relationship you put away two tubs of Ben & Jerry's every night watching Netflix.
- Maybe you make enough money to retire, but then you are bored and rudderless.
- Maybe you desired to have a child for oh so long, and then they come along and create a whole new world of chaos everyone warned you about but about which you had *no* idea.
- Maybe you become such a committed parent to your child that you forget who *you* are and put your own needs to the bottom of the pile, beneath the dog's.
- Maybe you desire to spend lots of time with your family as they grow up, but then you spend so much time with them that your earning capacity reduces, the kids take you for granted and you desire more variety in your life.
- Maybe you want to set up your own business then you go from a 40-hour-a-week job working for someone else to an 80-hour-a-week job working for yourself. Maybe you leave a company only to find that you don't like the people or the culture at the new employer.

In other areas of your life, those voids – perhaps linked to your greatest pain – never do get filled. And so we strive our whole life for more and more and more money, adrenaline-fuelled life experiences, sexual partners, success, love, respect and adulation. In these lifelong pursuits we experience temporary moments of fulfilment, and then the voids reopen and off we go searching again. This doesn't have to be a curse; it can be a great gift. This is what drives Elon Musk to build batteries and rockets. It's what drove Steve Jobs to relentlessly perfect and innovate. It's what drove Thomas Edison through 10,000 experiments to discover the lightbulb. It's what drove Oprah and Sir Tom Hunter and Sheryl Sandberg ... These voids drive all human progress.

You're faced in every moment with the paradox between striving for more and being happy and grateful for where you are. You're faced in every moment with the internal struggle between short-term cheap happiness and longer-term more fulfilling happiness. You're faced in every moment with the wrestling between your already being a unique, deserving human being and the void that drives you to become the person you want to be.

I don't profess to know the meaning of life, but the continual management of the push-pull of these opposing forces is likely to keep you in a more sustainable balance of both growth and satisfaction. These balanced outlooks should help you:

- be content with your continual desire for more
- be equally selfish and selfless
- set goals and enjoy the journey
- celebrate the small wins and the failures as well as the big goals
- be both future focused and present in the moment
- embrace order and chaos, control and letting go, accepting and demanding

- love the money, the game and the giving
- know you are worth more, and that you are already enough.

I would like to end this penultimate part of the book with a reflection on a real-life superhero of mine. I think Christopher Reeve, whose heroic life is a lesson to all of us, summed up so much when he said that 'a hero is an ordinary individual who finds strength to persevere and endure in spite of overwhelming obstacles'.

Reeve's journey of self-worth and discovery, including the struggles along the way, has helped so many of us develop lasting knowledge of who we are. Rest in Peace Christopher Reeve. You still inspire me today as much as you did when I was a child. Thank you for helping me and so many others honour who we are.

PART 6

Self-worth = net worth

54
Your worth is your wealth

The more you value yourself, the more the world values you. The more you invest in yourself, the more the world invests in you.

If you feel worthy, you are wealthy. Your wealth might be in your relationships, compassion, hobbies or sports, area of specialized knowledge, your children, or in whatever you hold to be of highest value and have therefore continually focused on. If you are not yet financially wealthy, you simply haven't learned, or connected with, how to convert that wealth into cash yet. There are millions of people across the planet who have done this: rock bands, artists, chefs, chocolatiers, designers, inventors, dog trainers, puppeteers, Lego builders, darts players, horse whisperers … Pick any weird and wonderful niche and someone has converted it into millions.

If they can all do it, you can do it.

I have a confession: for years I didn't know how to do it.

Since a very young age my dad had me working for money. He'd get me to 'bottle up' early mornings in his pub and would pay me £1 a week. Child labour, right ha! He would give me occasional one-off jobs for higher pay, and he'd challenge and reward me with money if I studied or worked hard.

As I grew up I looked for short cuts. The main ones involved asking my dad for money without working for it. I know he tried really hard not to just give me money, and instead teach me the value of earning money, but he had a really hard upbringing where he'd be given nothing (except bread and dripping, as he'd always tell me). Because of this he was occasionally a soft touch with me and would give me money if I asked.

Of course, once I worked out that there was this short cut, I relied on it much more than actually working for the money. And once my dad realized I'd worked this out, he got more frustrated with me asking for money. I'd then feel guilty about asking for money, but still didn't want to do the hard work required to earn it. It would get to the point where my dad would get angry with me asking for money, I'd feel awkward about asking for it, and occasionally he just pull the money out from his back pocket and throw it on the floor. He'd shout, 'There you go. Just bloody have it', and I'd have to pick it up off the floor in an apologetic manner.

Of course, there were a lot of unconscious things going on here. My dad was just carrying his emotions from the past, how he was treated and felt around money, and then bringing it into the current situation. I quite often caught him at times that were very inconvenient to him, or when he was very busy or stressed, so those emotions would be dumped out on to me.

I'd then experience my own emotions around money such as guilt, fear and shame. When these emotions are strong, they create chemical memories in the mind and body, fixed neural networks that create a habit. A habit is simply a pattern of emotions that have been felt repeatedly so that they become automatic.

So each and every time, even in adulthood, I wanted money from others I felt the same emotions. But this wasn't the current reality; this was the past reality playing out in the present moment. Just *thinking* about asking for money would create these emotions in my mind.

As I grew up this totally inhibited me around money. The emotions grow ever stronger because of the compounding effect, to the point where I'd completely stop asking for money. I painted and created art, but I'd never take my works to a gallery or make attempts to sell my work. I did everything I could to protect myself from the strong negative emotions, and therefore never put myself in any position where I had to ask for money, even as a fair return for work.

To make it worse I would focus all my time in non-productive areas, convincing myself that things would get better, never facing the reality that to make more money I would have to challenge the strong feelings. I simply painted more if my previous paintings didn't sell. I'd convince myself that things would be OK, which was a great lie. I was literally letting something that had happened when I was a child, more than 20 years before, jeopardize my entire future. The irony was that none of those current events were remotely like my childhood experiences, but I was turning these experiences into the painful experiences I'd had by imposing my past emotions on them.

Anyone who has strong negative (and sometimes positive) emotions around money is going to have their own version of this story. Before we move through this final part of *I'm Worth More*, it may help you to think of any incidents in your own past where you've had a difficult or negative experience around money, to which strong emotions have become attached? It could be ideals and beliefs about money passed down to you by your parents. It could be feelings of rejection or ridicule because your family had too little money – or even too much. This could be your reaction to someone wealthy whom you didn't like for some reason or other.

If you take time to consider this, you can literally go back to a specific time or event, or series of events, where all your blockages and resistance around money first stemmed from. When you realize that this wasn't something real, but merely your perception that formed your reality, you can change the meaning you took from this event.

I'll share some common money 'hang ups' in a moment, but first let's look at my experience of being both skint and wealthy …

55
I've been skint and I've been rich ...

We are all a product of our environment in the sense that we react to it. Our emotions are reactions and feedback to circumstances in our environment, and as such our beliefs, meanings, experiences and emotions around money come from the money related environments we have experienced.

Our experience is not the reality; it is just our reality. So whatever experience you've had around money can be changed by creating a different meaning and experience. Some people have been raised in an environment where money was hard to come by and where there were lots of painful experiences relating to money. They carry this experience forward into every present moment, thus manifesting their past experiences and beliefs into future situations. Others have been raised where money was easy, free and abundant. This has 'spoiled' some, but for many others it had made them value and appreciate it.

Most people in the world are not wealthy, yet they project their own beliefs and experiences as the 'reality' of money. We are all projecting out our own truths, trying to convince others of our truths. Of course, I am doing the same here, but I'm one of the few who has experienced both poverty and wealth – I've been skint and rich.

There are many skint people across the world who will tell you about the evils of money, when they've never even being wealthy. I've been raised by parents who were raised in first-world poverty, who yet gave me everything I needed and wanted, who worked so hard to give me a good life. Then from

18 to 25 years old I squandered that legacy and got myself into a lot of debt. I became entitled and ungrateful. That turned into bitterness and resentment, which I projected out on to anyone who had money. I became addicted to those emotions. It is far easier and safer to criticize the wealthy, rather than admit that you're not living to your full potential.

But I managed to get myself out of this vicious cycle, in part by luck, in part by serendipity and in part by a desire that had been in me since my early days of looking up to my dad. I read books on money and autobiographies of the wealthy and successful. I attended courses and masterminds. I started hanging around with and learning from the rich. I wrestled with my previous emotional memories and habits, and things started to change.

I paid off £50,000 of consumer debt and bought 20 properties with none of my own money, all within one year. I became financially free in my mid to late twenties and a millionaire between the ages of 30 and 31. I remember feeling slightly miffed as my target was to be a millionaire by 30. I then became a deca-millionaire and grew my companies until they had more than £100 million in turnover.

I write this with a small amount of fear based on my past experiences and feelings of vulnerability, because I know that some may judge me. But I also challenge myself to write this and put it out there, because I know others will love me for it. Some will hate about me the very thing that's great about me, and others will accept me for who I am.

I've been skint and I've been rich. I've done an accurate split test over decades of experience. I can categorically, unequivocally, state that being rich is far better than being skint. While I am by no means perfect and have many flaws, I much prefer the person I am now. I am considerably happier. I'm fortunate to be in a position to give far more to others, in the forms of time, experience and money. I pay considerably more tax than I have ever paid, and in many forms. My companies generate business rates, VAT, National Insurance for employers and employees, corporation tax, income tax in the millions and millions. I help, inspire and educate far more people than I did when I was skint. My self-worth is considerably higher. My vision is grander and my legacy is bigger.

Money has made me a better person. Money has taught me many valuable lessons. I value even more than the money, the lessons and experience that making, managing and mastering money have given me. Money has been the gift that keeps on giving and seems to never stop.

Of course, being rich has its downsides: responsibility, critics, trolls and haters, extra security, higher insurance premiums, more to lose, more people judging you. But this is the cost, and it's a cost I'm more than happy to pay. For me, the cost of being skint was my happiness, my self-worth and my confidence … There were people and experiences I never reached because of the money I didn't have.

Your experiences have made you who you are, and I'm not judging that. I'm simply saying you don't have to hold on to the experiences around money that deny you wealth and happiness. You can take control. You can change the past experiences and meanings. You can make money mean whatever you want it to mean, because we are all making meaning based on our experience, not the reality.

Money is neither good nor evil. Money does not judge. Money has no guilt nor shame. Money is simply money. It is humanity that gives it its meaning, purpose and function. Money is as malleable as the mind – a tool to create whatever you want.

So how much do you want it and what past experiences are you prepared to let go to get it?

56
Self-worth × network

Many people say that your 'network equals your net worth'. I'd refine that by saying your self-worth multiplied by your network equals your net worth.

All money in the world circulates via other people. People are the conduit of money – it flows from them to you, from you to them back to you and through you. This is why your network equals your net worth. The more people you know with money, or who have friends with money, the better the chance it will flow your way.

If the net worth of the people with whom you spend your time is negative, then yours is likely to be similar. Our behaviours are heavily influenced by people around us. We often unconsciously model our behaviour on theirs. In addition to this, there is the practical aspect of abundance or scarcity. If there is a scarcity of money flowing *around* us, it can't flow *to* us. If there are billions flowing to and through people, perhaps one or two stages removed in our network, it is far more likely to flow our way.

After all, money is simply a transfer of energy. You can't feel the heat of a fire a thousand miles away. Money is an exchange of value. Money is the physical measure of value and worth, converted into currency. The word 'currency' comes from the Latin verb for to flow or to run.

You convert latent value and worth into something physical. At first, the energy is in the form of an idea, solution, product or service. That energy gets converted into something physical that can be exchanged into currency. The money that flows to you is in equal balance to the quality, size, value and scale of the solution or product, under a fair exchange environment that equalizes your profit with their perceived value.

Your self-worth is the unconscious driver of this energy exchange. Your self-worth is transferred as energy into passion and the production of your product. Then into the marketing message and sales process around the work you do. Then on to and into the people you connect with, manifesting itself as the belief that you are worthy of being around. Then into the fair exchange process of pitching, pricing and persuasion that attracts money in equal exchange and measure.

Low self-worth is a lower-frequency energy exchange. You can't light a fire if you don't strike the match. When self-worth increases, it kick-starts a higher energy exchange which ripples out into production, people, pricing and persuasion – all required to make a sales exchange, whether in the form of a salary, loan or income from assets or selling.

As you attract money in fair exchange for your energy and value output, your self-worth determines how you receive and manage that money. People who value money least tend to give it away to people who value money the most. A person with low financial self-worth will either be bad at receiving money, and/or drive money away in the form of spending habits, addictions and liabilities, in an attempt to support or temporarily boost self-worth.

You can keep filling the bucket with water, but if you don't plug the hole, the bucket never fills. This goes some way to explaining why many people get into the trap of continually spending more than they earn, despite often earning good money.

57
Some common money hang-ups

In this chapter I look at some of the most common money-related hang-ups shared by people from all walks of life. You may see some of these beliefs and experiences in yourself or in others. None of them, remember, are real, but based on negative experiences to which you have attached negative emotions and behaviours.

1. **You stay in a relationship, partnership or dependency because you fear not having (enough) money**
   Many people have become comfortable, reliant or trapped in a partnership or relationship where they are not the main money earner. Over time they build up the belief that they can't earn their own money without the partner and get themselves stuck.

   In any relationship or partnership, of course you have to leverage out responsibilities and tasks, but there's nothing to stop you developing your own money management skills, your own sources of income and your own hedges against an uncertain future.

   If you know a partnership or relationship is wrong, don't trap yourself in it forever because you feel you have no other choice. Know that money is an abundant, almost infinite resource, and know that you have unlimited earning potential if you know your own worth, and learn to manage and master money.

2. You never spend money through fear of not having enough in the future

Hoarders, savers and stashers of money have a scarcity mindset around money. They may have experienced past losses and pains, or they may have been raised in a money-scarce environment. While saving and managing money are important, this can lead to paranoia or such tightfistedness that no one will want to give you money. The world will give more to a giver, and money needs to flow to function fully. Heightened cautiousness and reluctance to use your money can promote the fear that it's all you'll have and you won't get more in the future, whereas money is an almost infinite resource.

Sometimes you have to invest and speculate to accumulate. Sometimes you have to spend a little more to attract even more. Sometimes you have to give to receive.

3. You accept low money standards

If we have low self-worth, we may accept low money standards, such as taking work that is beneath us, a salary that doesn't match our skills or experience, doing free or cheap work for other people or companies that makes no profit or, worse, a loss. We might hang around other people who have low money worth, thus cementing further our lower standards.

We may feel that there will be no work, or that we will miss out, or, worse, that we will be left with no money, when in fact we are blocking higher-value jobs, salaries and fees because we are so busy dealing with lower-value work. The lesser blocks the greater, and you become known for lower-value work and hence you attract more of the same. A high worth and a feeling of deserving better, if not the best, around money means that you won't put up with, or stand for, things that reduce your worth or lower your standards.

4. You have extreme emotions and addictions relating to money

We tend to spend money on things we value the most, and our values are often areas where we have voids in our life we are trying to fill. For example, if health and well-being are highest on our values it may be because we lack the health and wellbeing we desire. We will prioritize spending money so that we look and feel better, often using money we don't have.

If you give a gambler or an alcoholic more money, what do you think they will do with that money? If you give a philanthropist more money, what do you think they will do with the money?

People often use spending to alleviate pain, whether that's via retail therapy or the thrill of exhilarating experiences. This is fine if balanced well and money is budgeted and managed, but many people have no control over this. Become aware of your emotions and addictions, which we all have, especially if you are using money you can't afford, to satiate these. Take control of your emotions and addictions and you will take control of your money.

5. You have issues relating to money you have inherited, borrowed or were gifted

People can feel a great sense of fear and responsibility managing money borrowed, gifted or inherited. This can turn into feelings of being undeserving, which can lead to paranoia about losing it. They may hold on to emotions connected to the donor, feeling pressure to live up to expectations or use the money wisely. This pressure can turn to stress and anxiety, which can lead to their doing nothing with the money, or, worse, making bad money judgements, such as giving the money to others to manage without due diligence.

At the other extreme, I've seen many people get loans, re-mortgage houses and enter joint-venture partnerships, where the money wasn't theirs, become flippant with their decision-making, cut corners and not take their responsibilities seriously enough.

The solution to both of these contrasting money issues is simple: act and behave as though you did earn it. Treat money with the utmost respect, and learn to manage and master it.

6. **You spend on others to buy their love and attention or heal them or yourself**

Many people desire to be liked and loved. We all crave attention. It is quite common for people to use money in an attempt to fill these voids. We literally try to buy people's love and acceptance. If this is something you can relate to, the best thing you can do is find other ways to gain love that aren't as expensive – the most simple of which is to spend time with people you love and who appreciate you for who you are.

You could also do other things to win people's love, such as acts of kindness, help and support, and other non-material things that may have even deeper value. There's nothing wrong with you if you desire love from people, but don't use money to gain this love. It can sometimes be a veil for a need to control people and can become addictive and manipulative.

7. **You believe that, if you have more money, others will have less**

When I've written articles or posted on social media about money, it's not uncommon for people to comment that the rich take from the poor, and that those who have vast amounts of money are depriving others of it.

This, however, isn't the reality of money. Money tends to flow from those who value it least to those who value it most. The (first-world) poor, who spend all their money due to volatile emotions and poor money management (which is not always their fault), aren't forced to hand over their money to companies. They did so through choice. Consumers hand over money to producers.

In addition, the perception that the rich are taking from those less fortunate is to assume that money only flows once – that, once spent, money can never be re-earned, which, of course, is not the case. Many skint people have earned well; they've just spent even better.

The reality always is that money will find its way back to those who know how to manage it, master it, create and produce and offer value in exchange for it.

8. You're not a good receiver of money

As strange as this may sound, many people are not good receivers of money. They may be fiercely independent and feel as though they have to be in control of everything themselves and never receive any help. They may see receiving as a weakness, or they may have guilt around receiving money from others in the form of gifts, loans, salaries and fees.

Many people offer their services for free that they should charge for. Many people undercharge or work for a lower salary, because they don't feel worthy of it or feel they may be judged for it.

When you are not a good receiver of money, you deny others the opportunity to help you (which is a gift to them). You deny the true nature of money, which is to ceaselessly flow. The more grateful a receiver of money you are, the more you will receive.

9. **You give your money away out of guilt, shame or not feeling deserving enough**

Often linked to a bad receiver of money is the desire or need to give all your money away. This can be in the form of charity donations, over spending, spending on others, a lack of budgeting and emotional or addictive spending.

Any number of emotions may underlie and fuel this need. There could be guilt of having money when you may not feel worthy or deserving of it. Maybe you came into money without working hard, and this conflicts with your values. You could feel judged, or that money may change you or that you are in some way depriving others. You may feel it isn't right to have an excess of money when so many people in the world have such a lack of it. You may not have forgiven yourself for past mistakes and emotional events, and the giving away of money is a kind of healing process for you.

Refer to all the points in this chapter to help you overcome these fears, doubts and negative emotions. Imagine all the great things you can do for yourself, your family and the wider world the more money you have. If you believe there should be more good in the world, use the money you have to do more good. Learn to hold on to and manage your money well, so you can pass that teaching as a gift to others.

10. **You 'over-control' money**

Many people feel they have to overly control situations, especially regarding money. This often arises out of a fear of failure, the desire and need for perfection, or experiences of being let down or screwed over in the past. The problem with this is you simply don't have enough time or resources to do everything yourself; you have to rely on other people to grow your wealth. You rely on your employer, your colleagues, your staff, your followers, your clients and your community. All money flows through people to people. So instead of grasping control you have to let go to grow.

Allow other people to take on tasks and responsibilities for you, and share the money. Leverage their time to get more done in less of your own time. Engage in partnerships and ventures which create more value. Great relationships with all these people will reduce the friction of money flow towards you.

A final note: if you find it hard to hold on to money and you give it all away, please send it all to me. I will graciously and gratefully accept all the money you want to give to make yourself feel better!

58
The formula for wealth

I strongly believe that we should all take control of and be fully responsible for the education, knowledge and management of (our own) money. Things go wrong when people don't know how to manage their emotions or decisions relating to money management. As a way to help further educate people on money (wealth), I created a formula for wealth based on almost 20 years' experience studying money, the wealthy, and turning my financial life around. The formula is:

$$W = (V + FE) \times L$$
Wealth = (Value + Fair Exchange) × Leverage

These final four chapters will first detail the wealth formula, and then the three parts in isolation, relative to self-worth. I will do my best not to duplicate too much content from my book *Money*, where this is one of the main subjects, and will try to explore it here in succinct form.

There are laws that govern money. The wealthy have studied and turned their experience into understanding and leveraging these laws. The (first-world) poor are unaware of these laws or, worse, are a victim to them. I state this with no moral judgement implied.

Because money tends to move from those who value it least, consciously or otherwise, to those who value it most, wealth will always move to those who know the laws. The formula for wealth is a formula I developed based on study, research and experience now spanning nearly two decades. The laws of wealth, illustrated in this formula, have stood the test of time, and have been consistent through every part of the economic cycle. The formula may look a little complicated but it is actually quite simple: you can leverage this formula for wealth just as much as anyone else.

Let's look at each part of the formula:

Value (V)

Value is the service you give to other people, as perceived by them. If you serve and solve, and show care and concern, then people will receive value and benefits that they will desire more of, pay for, and then refer you to others. It creates a knock-on energy transfer. People are looking for their problems to be solved, pains to be alleviated, and for things to be made faster, easier and better for them. Time is a scarce resource and a valuable commodity, so anything that leverages or preserves time will hold high value that is convertible into cash. If you're ever struggling financially or emotionally yourself, look more at how you can serve others and solve their problems, and you will have part of the formula for wealth solved, and more money will flow to you.

Your inner feeling of value (worth) will drive your outer creation of value, which will drive the perceived receipt of value. So you can't give value out to the world if you don't feel value in your inner world. This is the reason your self-worth equals your net worth, at least in relation to money. This is what stops you from applying for jobs offering twice your salary, because deep down you don't feel you are worth it. But it is also what stops you taking jobs at half your salary, because you don't think you are worth it (i.e. you feel worth more). This drives your pricing of your products, services and IP too.

Fair exchange (FE)

An exchange or transaction has to take place for you to receive money, leading to wealth. You have to offer a product, service or idea that someone else perceives valuable enough to pay for, and you have to be open and have high enough self-worth to receive a fair payment. This payment should include a fair and sustainable profit margin, otherwise it is unsustainable. When you gratefully receive financial (or other) fair compensation, you have a fair transaction, and repeat business and referrals are the result. Your gratitude will convert to value, and that will be perceived by the buyer.

Value without (fair) exchange (or a transaction), will create a financial void in your life, because you will be giving but not allowing receipt. There will be unfair exchange, you will have high overheads to revenue ratios, and your business and personal income will be unsustainable. You will also build resentment and bitterness. Guilt, lack of confidence, imposed religious or social beliefs, perceived market ceilings and extreme emotions make a transaction too one-sided and unsustainable. This could be in the form of not charging or pricing too low; overly favouring the buyer. This will have a knock-on effect of a reduction in value creation, which will create a vicious cycle.

On the other extreme, if you charge prices that are unfairly high, relative to the value you give, you will be perceived as unfair, greedy or worse ripping people off. You may be able to temporarily surge sales because of a big claim or a false promise, or merely a naive lack of commercial experience, but it will reverse once the reality of the lack of value is perceived. In the end, your overheads will rise as you have to compensate in the forms of extra customer service, refunds, PR, damage limitation or law suits. This is also unsustainable for the long-term, and could lead to insolvency.

Leverage (L)

Leverage is the scale and speed of service and remuneration, and the impact it has. The more people you can serve and solve their problems, the more money you make. It could be the number of customers, followers and fans. It could be the volume of referrals and repeat transactions through multiple purchases and customer loyalty. It could be higher prices and margins. It is your reputation, brand, and the spreadable, sharable nature of your enterprise or marketing message. It is the local to national to global reach and impact you have.

Also, the bigger the problem, the higher the transactional amount (as fairness is dictated by the scale and size of the problem). The more valuable the product, service or offer, the more satisfied it makes people, and the quicker it will spread virally. You've probably noticed that your highest paying customers are often your most grateful customers and take the least amount of customer service.

You will only leverage and scale wealth for the long term if you have value *and* fair exchange. You could get transient spikes and viral sharing of a big claim or promise, but anything that doesn't serve and solve won't continue to scale. Once unfair exchange is discovered, like you are not doing a good enough job but you are on a good salary, you will be humbled and brought back into balance. In fact, it can be very dangerous to scale too fast, because what is broken will exaggerate, compound, and things may start to break if you are not prepared for the chaos of scale. Also, if you are promising undeliverable value, that will exacerbate with scale. Your overheads will increase and margins may even go negative. This is why you hear smart business advisors suggest not to scale too early or quickly, and that businesses can be profitable but run out of cash, or where they have been a great business for many years but one big problem wipes them out.

Focus on the three parts to the formula equally, but in the right order (Value, then Fair Exchange, then Leverage) and hire or partner with the best people in the two areas you are personally weaker at. You can then take on the part you enjoy the most. Once you fix or build whichever part of the formula is broken or not created yet for you, the floodgates for wealth and net worth can open up. You need to keep testing, taking feedback and tweaking as you scale. What worked will change. Economies and markets will evolve, and new challenges will present themselves perennially. If you embrace this rather than become a victim to this constant evolution, it gives you the best competitive advantage you could wish for.

Now let's go into each element (V, FE and L), one per chapter.

59
Value (V)

Value is a three-way fine balance between:

- you living your values, *and*
- the things you value that allow you to grow and self-actualize, so that you feel valuable inside, *and*
- giving external, high perceived value to others.

When you get this balance right, you are more able to merge your passion and profession, do what you love, love what you do, help others and make money.

It is the fine balance between meeting your selfish desires, and being selfless in giving value to others. These are all inter-linked: when you give value to others, that cements your own feeling of value. When you do something 'selfish' for yourself, you also feel more valuable and full, which then reflects outwards to the value you offer to others.

I think this can best be explained by my own experience of helping myself, helping others and monetizing that through a training and education business.

My training companies generate tens of millions in sales and are a viable business model that allows me a good lifestyle. These businesses employ almost 100 staff, generate millions in tax, help many families pay their overheads, and support chari-ties and even a foundation, the Rob Moore Foundation.

If the companies gave too much value, and didn't have a fair exchange pricing strategy or revenue model, it wouldn't be able to sustain and grow, and contribute in all the above areas. It is a commercial venture and not just a selfless act, and the commercial is required to sustain the overheads of giving value.

If it didn't give enough value, there would be resistance, complaints, increased overheads or worse reputational and legal battles, which also carry significant cost.

So the founders of this company, or any company, need to balance the selfish and selfless, commercial and contribution, for maximum growth.

I got into training for both selfish and selfless reasons. Selfishly it feels really good to help other people; make no mistake about it, I experience a purely selfish feeling of feeling more valuable when others are grateful for what I've done for them. This become addictive and then fuels more value creation.

But this has a time cost, which has a financial cost that needs to be covered. So a company is formed, courses are created and charges levied to cover these overheads and make a profit. Zero profit is either a failed business, hobby or charity. This profit then self-fulfils into a higher feeling of self-worth as money comes in. Money appreciates and you appreciate money; and what you appreciate appreciates. You get more satisfaction and more money, which feeds your selfish interests and serves the market in a balanced, selfless way.

If you don't have confidence in your own value, you won't put that value out to the world, and won't assign fair prices to that work. The world won't be able to get value and therefore won't appreciate you. More on that in the fair exchange section.

If you don't value yourself, no one else will value you, and you won't have confidence to put value out to the world. You can't give out what you don't have inside.

The ways you can increase the way you value yourself relative to money are:

1. **Go back to the events in your past where you had poor relationships with money, or money-related events, and see the upsides of how they served you.**

   They don't define you, they are merely past events that you have carried forward as a habit that predict your future. Forgive yourself for another's perceived wrongs regarding money and see how it can serve you to make you more of a money magnet.

   For example, if you perceive someone screwed you over for money, and that's created money trust issues ever since, go back and get all the lessons from the experience: your lack of due diligence, what you learned about human behaviour, technical aspects such as security and charges and contracts.Carry what you have learned forward to achieve better financial transactions in the future.

2. **Commit to learning about the laws of money.**

   Money is predictable when you fully understand the concepts surrounding it. Money is merely a universal exchange of value and measurable unit of account. It is a way to more efficiently exchange goods, products and services in a measurable way without delay. It is a way to measure or score, save, invest or hedge for an uncertain future.

   Money tends to move from those who value it least to those who value it most. Money is a human construct and thus follows the actions, reactions and emotions of people, not of money itself. Money only has manifest meaning when you, the individual, place your values and beliefs on to it.

The more you know, the more you grow. The more you learn, the more you earn. Commit to constant reading of money, observing the wealthy, listening to podcasts, attending courses and remaining a humble student of money for your entire life.

3. **Learn to love, appreciate and be grateful for money.**
Gratitude is easy when things are great, but in order to attract more money you need to be grateful for every financial exchange. That includes bills and debts. Be grateful giving it and grateful receiving it.

4. **Expect wealth, for it is your right.**
Expectation theory states that you get what you expect, not what is apparently 'fair' or what you 'deserve'. You are worthy of wealth and money. It is your right, as it is for all. No one was born destined to be poor, and we are all supposed to self-actualize; money is an enabler of your higher, wealthier self. Expect to be wealthy both in the form of giving and creating, and allowing it to come through you. Are you valuing all of your life's effort and work in your fees, charges and salary requests? Everything you have done in your life should be reflected in your worthiness, and it will lead to a vast net worth. Recount all the things you've done and experienced in your life; go back as far as you can, and list as many things as you can that would add value to your worth, both in your personal feeling of worthiness and as value to contribute to others. This could be education, degrees, awards, earning, creations and contributions. Focus on what you have and not what you lack. Focus on what you can do and not what you can't.

5. **Consider who you spend time with and, if necessary, make changes.**

The truth behind the phrase 'your network is your net worth' is that you are the sum of the five people you spend the most time with. If you spend time with five skint people on a regular basis, you will likely become that. If you spend time with five billionaires on a regular basis, you will likely become that, because you will consume yourself in that new reality and you will become your environment.

It is categorically your choice who you spend the most time with. Do you want to be lifted up or dragged down? You can make the choice to spend time with successful wealthy people who elevate you, who educate, motivate and inspire you, who open you up to new possibilities, give you new experiences, insight and support. You will learn their money models, systems, money management tactics, behaviours and emotions, leverage strategies and investments. This can be in the form of mentors, peers, masterminds, friends of friends who you can get wise counsel from, or people you study in books, at events and via documentaries. One of the greatest gifts my podcast gives to me is the amazing, wealthy and successful people I meet. It literally pulls me up and cracks open my mind, vision, belief and energy.

60
Fair exchange (FE)

When I was an artist, my art was cheap. That wasn't because it was crap (before you say it). And it wasn't because I'm from Peterborough and Dad is a Northerner from Huddersfield either. I'd convinced myself it was because people in Peterborough didn't have any money. I knew the canvas and material costs, and as those costs were low, it felt greedy to charge high London prices. I'd typically sell a 1m × 1m canvas for £495. By typically, I actually mean very rarely. Someone could easily get me down to £350 – all they had to do was breathe. If it hadn't sold for a long time I'd probably drop to £250 or even £200. If it was sold in a gallery, then the gallery owner would take 40 per cent, so I'd be left with between £120 and at best £300. I charged the same for five years so inflation would have eaten away at those figures by the end of 2005. I just couldn't get my head around charging more. I considered trying to sell my work in London after entering a couple of competitions. After not getting any recognition, I went right back into my shell feeling that London was too self-righteous. Plus it was an embarrassing experience to take huge canvasses by hand on, the London Underground knowing that I couldn't really afford the four-way train fare to take it, come back, then pick it up when I 'lost' and bring it back again.

The story about Picasso describing a napkin sketch as the culmination of a life's work changed my approach entirely. There it was, right in front of me like a sumo-slap in the face; the clearest explanation as to why I was significantly under charging for my work. I was only valuing the cost of the materials, and not the time, investment, total cost, opportunity cost, awards and degrees, commitment, pain, passion and dedication to art since I was three years old. That was over 20 years of experience I wasn't valuing or pricing in to my work. The message is strong. Your prices must include your life's work, education, experience, desire to serve, solve and care, and the sacrifices you've made. If they don't, then you'll experience the feelings I felt of guilt, embarrassment, bitterness and lack of self-worth. You'll resent your buyers for paying a lower price that, ironically, you set. Of course value is subjective and relative, so the value as perceived by the buyer is also part of the value-determining, fair exchange process. You can't just slap a huge price tag on if the seller doesn't think it is fair either. *It is this balance of fair value and fair price that creates fair exchange.*

An exchange (or transaction) has to take place for you to receive money and wealth. Otherwise it is a hobby or charity. You give a product or service that someone perceives has value to them so they willingly exchange payment in equal value for it. Fair exchange is a minimum, usually two-way exchange between a buyer and seller, or an employer and employee. For fair exchange to take place the seller must add value as perceived by the buyer, and the buyer must exchange equal monetary value as perceived by the seller. Only under fair exchange do you have free monetary flow, and therefore wealth. A market or an individual governs the perceptions of fair exchange, sometimes separately, like art, sometimes in unity, like the price of fuel. Prices always tell the truth, because they are the agreement between what they seller will accept and the buyer will pay.

Value without (fair) exchange or remuneration isn't actually value at all. *Most people don't value what they don't pay for.* Have you ever been given a book for free that's got dusty on the shelf? You may have increased your 'shelf-development', but free advice is worth every penny and most people don't value it. Imagine if you paid £500 for a book. Would you read it then? Value is a perception that money quantifies and puts something ethereal into a tangible and specific measurement.

Many poor (skint) people who struggle to make significant wealth don't realize they're actually creating and attracting scarcity by pricing their products and services too low. I now know that's what I did. I thought that there wasn't anyone in Peterborough with any money to buy my art, when in fact the inverse was happening. My low-priced art was attracting low-paying customers. Even worse was that it was repelling higher-paying ones. I had guilt, fear and worry about pricing my work higher. In turn, I devalued my self-worth and worth the world gave to me. I felt unfair exchange was happening to me, when in reality I was creating unfair exchange myself.

If you don't price highly enough, no one will volunteer to give you more money than they perceive to be 'fair', just to help you with higher, fairer pricing. No one is going to give you more money just to lift your self-worth. That has to come from you. If you price too low your fees or salary, the fair exchange balance will be out, and there will be consequences of unsustainability in the form of zero or negative profit, and resentment from the seller or employee. Zero margin and resentment will perpetuate a lower self-worth and poorer relationships with clients and employers. The buyer, in turn, will perceive a lack of value, despite paying a low price. This attracts more of the same because of the laws and nature of money. Ironically the solution is so very simple. Put your prices, fees and salary requests up!

Because money reflects and serves humanity, which is an amazing paradoxical balance, the other extreme of unfair exchange is also unsustainable. Examples of illegal or unfairly gained wealth are often cited as a counter to fair exchange, and more for a need for power. Perhaps it is true for the short-term that you can make money dealing in drugs or running the government of a depraved communist society, but these are extreme and rare examples. If you study history, you will find most of these instances of excessive greed and power are unsustainable, and the consequences are often in line and scale with the greed. The balanced result could be huge debt, prison or worse. Anyone who exerts excessive power for gains more towards the self than the whole of humanity usually gets unseated, overthrown or, in extreme cases, killed.

So, if receiving occurs without fair giving, or someone offers a product, service or idea and the remuneration is too high (or value too low), there will be consequences. People will feel disappointed, ripped off or worse: conned. They will spread the message aggressively, which will affect your reputation and reduce future sales. A good message will be shared four times and a bad one eleven times, according to 'The secrets of word-of-mouth marketing'. Sales may, at first, spike until the lack of value has been proven, and then it will reverse because the price exceeds the market ceiling, or there was a lower per-ceived value than the level of remuneration. In extreme cases the perception will be ripping off, conning or outright theft. And it can be over a low-value item, like Ryanair flights. Rya-nair changed strategy in the end due to aggressive complaining; they were literally forced back into balance and better service.

It is important to observe both extremes of fair exchange, and strive to strike balance. Wealth is momentum and velocity of the laws of money in action, and you can only build and sustain it through continued fair exchange. Too much extreme in favour of the self and perceived value to others is reduced. Too much extreme in favour of others, and worth and sustain-ability of the self are reduced.

PayPal realized that sending money by email was going to be massive, that one company would dominate it, that it was relatively easy to do, and that nobody dominated it *yet*. They quickly tried various things as a route to market. Initially, they provided no incentives or value for customers to join their services, and that was their biggest challenge. They needed organic, vigorous growth. So they gave customers money. New customers got $10 for signing up, and existing ones got $10 for referrals. Growth went exponential, and PayPal increased the gift to $20 for each new customer. Their flexibility and increased value, first, proved to be a major asset. PayPal was swift enough to change course in time to go public in 2002 and was later bought out by eBay for $1.5 billion. A recent estimation of PayPal's valuation was around $50 billion, all off the back of giving first.

As you operate under fair exchange, you increase your self-worth because you feel adequately remunerated for your time and work. This, in turn, helps you increase your prices and value. You are able to make a profit, which means you can increase the scale of your service and reinvest back into quality and value. Furthermore, as you increase your prices and value, you attract a better quality of customer who values what you offer, and is willing to pay more. As they pay more you can give and serve more, creating a virtuous cycle of growth and contribution, increasing the velocity of money and augmenting its nature. This is another reason why increasing your prices is important. This would have saved me nearly five years of my life and £50,000 debt had I been able to read this when I started out as an artist. Tracey Emin sold *My Bed* for £2.2 million. Damien Hirst sold *Lullaby Spring* for £9.65 million. I sold sweet FA and was a bitter bastard for many years.

61
Leverage (L)

Leverage is achieving more, with less: more money with less, or other people's money, more time with less time, or less of your personal time and more results with less effort, or less of your personal effort. Leverage is reach, scale and impact, at speed. Heed the words of the great engineer Archimedes: 'Give me a lever long enough and I could move the world.'

Most people are unleveraged, conditioned to believe that 'working harder' means you'll earn more money. You have to 'graft' and 'sacrifice' in order to 'earn a living'. *Living is your right, you don't have to 'earn' it, you should be living it.* Everyone experiences leverage: servant or master, employer or employee, leader or follower, lender or borrower, consumer or producer. Each serves the other, but one leverag*es* and the other is leverag*ed*. You're either utilizing leverage, moving towards your inspired vision, earning on other people's time, money, resources, network, systems, experience, skills, or you are being leveraged to serve someone else's grand vision.

If you work for someone else and you're not happy, or you work for money and that money stops when the work stops, then you are being controlled by the leverage of others. They are earning from you, you're lower down the value chain, earning less yet you're working hard. You probably have the least control and freedom, and you're possibly unhappy. Most people are made to believe that time, work and money are directly related. Millionaires, billionaires and visionaries know they are inverse. You're taught to work hard for money, but you need make your money work hard for you. You're taught that longer hours and overtime earn more money, but in reality, vision, leverage, leadership and building your network and team to fulfil these actually creates vast and lasting wealth.

Millionaires, billionaires or simply good money managers earn money and preserve time on other people's time, resources, knowledge and contacts. Just take a look at the billionaire lifestyle. Are they really working 'harder' than the miners, servants and cleaners? No. Leverage is learnable and you can learn the same strategies and tactics they know, have learned, and are using to make money, preserve time and make a difference.

Leverage is easier than ever, due to the Internet, fibre optics and all the apps, media, tech and systems that leverage them. You can outsource most of your operational tasks, even if you are a one-man band. You can employ a virtual PA who you can pay by hour, to free your time to focus more on Income Generating Tasks (IGTs). You can leverage the various and vast social media channels for low cost or free reach to millions of people. You can become an influencer without TV and radio ads. You can become your own media empire of one with a phone camera, YouTube channel and podcast. You can use big data, intuitive algorithms and AI to react to the markets and your users in virtually real time. You can crowdsource ideas and content from your communities and social media groups. You can crowdfund start-ups and assets from the masses. You can leverage someone else's ideas like Steve Jobs did with existing tech. You can leverage information free and widely available.

If we moved through the industrial age into the information age, now we may be in the leverage age. One 'shout-out' or recommendation from an influencer and you could go viral.

Relative to the wealth formula, it's the speed and scale of the value exchange that matters. It is the increase in income and impact through growth, more connections, and increased visibility and reputation. Leverage is reach, scale and impact, at speed. No leverage, no visibility. No visibility, no existence in the wider markets and world.

In Chapter 6 (How *you* value something), I gave examples of innovative business models and passionate people who converted unique talents and passions into serious profits. You are already a millionaire, hundred-millionaire or billionaire, but in another, as of yet non-monetary, form. You just have to appreciate your talents so they appreciate. Convert your latent wealth into actual cash. The millionaire has converted their own values and uniqueness into monetary form, and you can too.

If these people can do it, what's to say you can't too? I'm sure they all had the same fears, doubts and concerns about monetizing their unique, strange and quirky business models, but they followed their passion and look where it took them. The four elements to turn your passion into your profession and your unique talents into cash are passion, profession, market and profit.

1. Passion

Passion is energy, enthusiasm, some hustle, problem-solving, relentless desire, often on a consistent and continual basis in the face of adversity. You and your business will be tested regularly, so the fire that continues to burn is your passion. If there is little or no passion, you will throw in the towel as soon as it gets difficult.

- Either look within and search for the passions you already have, or continue to ask every single day: 'What am I most passionate about?'

- 'What would I love to do for a very long time, even the rest of my life?'
- 'What would I do that I wouldn't consider work?'
- 'What would it be a privilege to have as my career?'

Start there.

Some people just know it from a very young age. Others have to keep testing, searching and struggling, but if you keep asking you will find it. You can start part-time evenings and weekends, or you can go all in, full time, that is your choice.

2. Profession

Profession is the commercialization of your passion. Your passion with no monetary element is either a charity or a hobby. In previous generations, professions were pretty set and monetizing a hobby or interest was virtually unheard of. In the modern world of the decentralization of media, the Internet, social media, influencers and personal branding, it is easier and more relevant than ever to monetize a 'hobby'. Factors you want to consider are: do you want to monetize this passion? Are you prepared to learn the commercial and business elements of this passion? Do you want to scale it, and use it as a way to help and serve others? If so, let's go!

3. Market

Market is the space and number of potential clients you can reach. If your grand vision is to run a colonic irrigation retreat in Outer Mongolia, that may not have a market big enough for you to scale. No idea why I selected that specific example! You'd want to know that there is a growing area of interest for your product and that it is not too hyper niche. Kevin Kelly, a futurist who I interviewed for my 'Disruptive Entrepreneur' podcast believes you only need 10,000 true followers or potential customers to have a good viable and sustainable business. It's easier than ever to do some down and dirty superfast research by checking Google trends, Google searches, what is trending on social media platforms, and keywords that have a good search volume. Innovators and disruptors often ignore this area, because they feel that their product or service will forge its own market. You can create demand by creating products and services people didn't even know they needed, but no harm in checking for market viability and scale first.

4. Profit

Profit is the final piece in the puzzle that most people miss. Profit is simply a monetary result of the wealth formula. It's the fair commercial transaction that cements the value of the product and service. It actually increases value, because we tend to value what we pay for and not what we get for free. The producer will be more accountable and committed to delivering the product and service which benefits the consumer. The consumer will be more accountable to use or consume the product because they've made a payment. So, you could argue a strong case that the payment is better service than non-payment. Payment exchange is also a guarantee. The money flow into transaction enables reinvestment into innovation and improved products and services. The money flow includes taxes, rates and contributions that are fed back into public services. The money flow creates employment, which generates further taxes and funds people's lifestyles and livelihoods.

Money is literally the idea, the vision, the creativity and the spiritual converted into the material. You are an alchemist of money when you honour your passion, turn it into a profession, serve a market and balance the wealth formula elements of value, fair exchange and leverage.

I believe you are worth far more than you are currently getting in monetary exchange. This is because you have unique talents and gifts, that have value to the world, latent within you that need to be expressed and unleashed. You have skills and things you find so easy, that others require as a solution to their problems and pains. What others struggle with and would pay for, you enjoy and find easy.

You have lived your whole life as an equally relevant human being to any other person on the planet. You are worth so much more, but it has to start with you. Please do not let this book be the end, but just the beginning of the gift you give to yourself and the world of appreciating yourself for who you are. You are already enough as you are, it's all there within you. You've lived your whole life and that should be factored into your work, your salary and your prices. Equally, you can continue to develop your skills, passion, understanding, knowledge, experience and your network further to ever increase your self-worth.

And always remember to say to yourself each and every time you feel down or lost …

'I'm worth more.'